Hearing The Voice

By
Ted J. Hanson

House of Bread Publishing
Bellingham, Washington

Hearing The Voice

© 2015 Ted J. Hanson

Paperback and e-book volume - 2015

House of Bread Publishing
3210 Meridian St., Bellingham, WA 98225

ISBN 978-0-9908251-8-0
Library of Congress Control Number: 2015954279

Cover By Amani Hanson - Becoming Studios
as per House of Bread Publishing
3210 Meridian St.
Bellingham, WA 98225

Editing contributions by Emilyanne Zornes, P-Come Proof&Copy

All Scripture quotations in this volume are from the *New King James Version* of the Bible, © 1982, Thomas Nelson, Inc.

Printed in the United States of America

About the Author

Ted J. Hanson has been a born again believer in Christ since May 12, 1973. He has served as a worship leader, youth leader, administrator, associate pastor, senior pastor, and is presently an apostolic minister to the Body of Christ throughout the world. He and his wife, Bonnie, reside in Bellingham, Washington.

Ted is an apostolic leader with a prophetic mantle. He is a dynamic preacher/teacher who has a heart to share, uncompromisingly, the Word of God and the Lordship of Jesus Christ. He holds a bachelors of theology and a masters of biblical studies through Christian International Ministries Network and is ordained through Abundant Life Ministries and House of Bread Ministry.

God has given Ted a vision for the liberty of the Spirit of God within the Church. Like Joshua, his vision is to see the Church come into the abundance of the inheritance of God. His heart is to equip God's people for the work of the ministry and see all come into the reality of the abundant life that Jesus came to give. He presently serves as an equipping and resource ministry to the body of Christ globally. He has developed and led School of Eagles Ministry Academy for training, equipping, and activating ministry in God's people. This is now known as Christ Life Training, an in class and online training school (www.christlifetraining.com).

Ted travels to various places throughout the U.S. as well as other countries. He not only ministers the Word of God and operates in the prophetic, he also activates others in prophetic ministry. He has served to plant and establish many ministries. He is part of Reformation International Ministries and provides apostolic training, direction, and counsel to many churches and ministries at home and abroad. His home church of Abundant Life was planted and established by Ted and is presently led by his son, Pastor Jonathan Hanson.

Ted has written several books, including *Spiritual Man, The New Testament Prophet, Properly Judging Prophetic Ministry, Prophetic Ministry – A Ministry of Life, The Redeemed Earth –Healing the Curse of the Fall, The Seven Eyes of Grace, Generational Leadership, Understanding Authority, For His Glory – You Have Been Left Behind, Christ Unveiled – A Revelation of Jesus Christ, and The NOW Covenant – Chist In You the Hope of Glory.* He also writes weekly blogs at *www.ted4you.com* and *www.ted4leaders.com*.

Contents

Preface

I have written this book in regard to Hearing God's Voice. My hope is that this book will inspire all who read it to recognize the voice of God in their hearts more clearly. My desire is that all who read this book will discover a deeper love for God, for themselves, and for their journey in life.

What is hearing God's voice? Is it a matter of knowing what to do in life, or is there something more? Does our view of who God is affect our ability to hear Him? What is the purpose of hearing Him? What is His desire for us in hearing Him? How do we hear Him? How does He speak? What does His voice sound like? How do my spirit, my soul, and my physical being influence my ability to hear God? Is hearing Him simple or hard? Do I hear Him immediately, or is there a process in hearing Him? How can I trust that what I am hearing is God?

I have been a believer in Christ for over forty-two years and I have learned many secrets to hearing God's voice. I have given my life to be a spiritual father in activating, facilitating, and releasing God's voice in the hearts of people. My wife and I raised our own children to hear God's voice and they have all grown to be healthy people who know the power of Christ within them and understand His voice clearly. I pastored a church for twenty years with a foundational value of helping each member grow in hearing God's voice in his or her life. I am now a spiritual influencer of the body of Christ nationally and internationally and hearing God's voice is at the core of all that I serve the body of Christ to know.

I have taught a course on hearing God's voice for fifteen years in my ministry training school, now known as Christ Life Training (www.christlifetraining.com). This book is based upon the things that I have taught in this course for the past fifteen years. I have studied God's word in depth concerning the subject of hearing God and I have sought to demonstrate my findings in the living testimony of my life, my family, and my responsibilities in the local church and to the body of Christ.

My purpose in writing this book has been to share from my heart secrets to hearing God and knowing His guidance. My aim is to help anyone who reads this book recognize God's voice in his or her own life and find the liberty of hearing Him. I hope to bring freedom from condemnation, shame, guilt, or any attribute of bondage that has somehow entered into the process of hearing God. I want to bring the freedom of relationship with God in the process of hearing Him.

I believe that this book will prove to be important for anyone who reads it. I believe it will prove to be an essential resource to those who are involved in leadership in church ministries of any kind. I also believe that this book offers essential secrets to life for any person in their daily walk as a human being. I believe that this book will inspire healthy marriages, healthy families, healthy churches, and healthy people in an everyday world.

I begin by presenting an introduction to the purpose of hearing God. Is hearing Him about knowing what to do? Does God want to talk to us? Is He speaking and am I hearing what He is saying? What is the key to hearing Him in my life? Does everyone hear God? Is hearing Him enough, or is there something more on my part? How does my view of who God is affect my ability to hear Him?

In the first chapter I present several foundations for hearing God. This chapter reveals how hearing God is connected to who we are. I present how shame affects our ability to hear God and how hearing God removes all shame from our lives. Hearing God brings faith. What does faith really look like? And how do we know that we have faith? How does faith work? Does it simply come by God speaking or is there an internal atmosphere where faith happens? God's words are life-giving words. How do we recognize the difference between words that bring life and words that bring bondage and control? Hearing God doesn't only bring faith, it produces faith and the things that happen because of faith. What is the purpose of true faith? What hinders faith? How do we overcome the hindrances to faith? God's words are kingdom words.

What do kingdom words sound like and what is the purpose of kingdom words? What is the kingdom of God and how do we discern words that promote God's kingdom? Hearing God gives us life. What is life? What is the process of life? How does hearing God relate to life?

Chapter 2 addresses how hearing God guides our lives. It begins with knowing God, not merely knowing what to do. Hearing God is intensely connected to God and it draws us closer to Him. It doesn't empower us to be independent from Him. What is the witness to God's guidance in our lives? What things resist God's guidance in our lives? How do we overcome those things that resist His guidance in our lives? How do we discover His guidance and how can we trust that we are hearing correctly? How does our perception of Him affect our responses to Him and our understanding of His voice in our lives? What hindrances do we need to be aware of when it comes to receiving God's guidance in our lives? What has God given that is a witness to His voice in our lives? How do we embrace His sure witnesses and apply them in the process of hearing God? How does guidance occur in our lives and how do we position ourselves to receive it? How does who we are affect our ability to receive His guidance?

Chapter 3 presents the process of God's guidance in our lives. There are many confirming witnesses in the process of hearing God. This chapter presents key elements in the process of hearing God and being led by Him in the journey of life. What about circumstances? How do circumstances play into the process of God's guidance in our lives? What about the peace of God? What is the peace of God and how do we recognize it?

In Chapter 4 you will see the importance of hearing God. An understanding of the purpose of hearing God will reveal the power of hearing God. Hearing God will overcome the gates of hell. What are the gates of hell and how are they overcome by hearing God?

Chapter 5 gives instructions in how to hear God's voice in your life. Who hears God's voice? Does everyone hear Him or only a few? If I am not hearing Him can I do something that will enable me to hear Him?

Chapter 6 shows how to recognize God's voice. God is Spirit. How does that play into the process of hearing Him? How do we hear God in our souls? Does He speak directly to our souls? How does being spirit, soul, and body play into the process of hearing Him? This chapter deals with this process and it will give you keys to growing in hearing God. What is the assurance of recognizing the process of hearing Him in our lives? How do we position our hearts to embrace the process of hearing Him?

Chapter 7 presents hindrances to hearing God. What are the strategies of the devil in warring against our souls? How does this affect our ability to hear God? What is the difference between the voice of the enemy and the voice of God? How do we recognize the voice of the enemy?

Chapter 8 reveals how our attitudes affect our ability to hear God. Our attitudes can be good or bad. How does our attitude enable us to hear God? I give examples of how the attitude has affected others' ability to understand what God was saying in their lives. Our attitude is key in hearing God.

Chapter 9 is about learning to do the will of God. Doing the will of God is the result of hearing Him. Is the will of God merely about doing what God says? How do we position ourselves to do His will? Then Chapter 10 reveals secrets to knowing what the will of God is. How does knowing the general will of God affect our ability to know the specific will of God? How do we receive the specific will of God in our lives? By what means does God reveal His specific will in our lives? This leads to Chapter 11, where I address specifically what the will of God is in our lives. How is this unique for each of us? How do we conclude what the specific will of God is? What methods does God use to show us His specific will? God's will is not informational; it is transformational. It doesn't just empower us to know what to do; it empowers who we are. This chapter gives essential keys to this process. Chapter 12 gives conclusive evidence to knowing, with confidence, the will of God in our lives. There is a process in reaching the knowing stage of God's will in our lives. This chapter reveals that process. It includes the beginning of hearing, the direction of hearing, and the wisdom of hearing that leads to the future in our lives. The differences between revelation, interpretation, and application will be explored. An appropriate equation of how these three things are involved in the process of God's guidance in our lives will be revealed.

In the final chapters I present a list of questions to ask, as a check to the voice of God in our lives. This list is a presentation of thoughtful questions based upon what I have presented in this book. The final chapter is a prayer that I have made for all reading this book in the belief that this book will help all who read it in hearing God, knowing God, and living a life in relationship with Him, hearing His voice.

This book can also be used as a resource to the class Hearing God's Voice, a class I have been teaching for many years in Christ Life Training (formerly School of Eagles). Online versions of this course can be found at the training website – www.christlifetraining.com. Bob Mumfort's book *Take Another Look At Guidance* [1] has been an inspiration for this course and for the concept of this book. I recommend this book as a supplicant to your understanding of hearing God.

In conclusion, reading this book will challenge and empower you to hear God, respond to Him, and become a testimony of Him in this world. The secrets revealed in this book are foundational for every believer in hearing God and walking a path of intimacy with Him in life. I consider this book essential for church pastors and leaders, so the church can embrace the realities of hearing God. I consider the book essential for those who believe they are apostles, prophets and teachers to the church at large. Hearing God should be a part of our love relationship with God. It is delightful and wonderful to know Him and to walk with Him in all things. I pray the Spirit of God opens the eyes of your understanding as you read the truths written within. I pray that the secrets revealed become an inheritance in your life for the generations that follow your walk in this world.

[1] Bob Mumford, *Take Another Look At Guidance* (Raleigh, NC: Lifechangers Publishing, 1971, 1972, 1973, 1974, 1993, 1999)

Introduction:

Hearing God To Know God

In this book I am going to address the subject of hearing God's voice and receiving His guidance in our lives. In order for us to hear God correctly we must have a proper foundation for hearing Him. God has granted us a New Covenant foundation in Christ. We have a NOW relationship with God and we can hear God in the NOW moments of our lives. We must embrace a New Covenant perspective to hear the voice of God in the New and NOW reality of His covenant with men.

The Old Covenant was a covenant based upon the knowledge of good and evil in a government of the knowledge of good and evil. It was not God's desire for men to be under a government of the knowledge of good and evil. That government was a result of man's own decision in the Garden of Eden. Man chose the knowledge of good and evil over an intimate relationship with God based upon love and trust. This left mankind thinking that knowing what to do was the most important thing in life. This still affects us today. We tend to think that hearing God is about knowing what to do in life. I propose that if hearing God is about knowing what to do, than knowing what to do is our god. I believe that hearing God is about knowing God. It isn't about knowing what to do. The worst thing in life is not to be wrong. The worst thing in life is to be dead. Hearing God brings us life and the power of transformation unto life. It doesn't merely bring information for direction in our lives. Hearing a person is about knowing that person, unless you are a slave and the person is your master. God is a Father, not a master of puppets or slaves! He is a Father who loves His children!

In a government of the knowledge of good and evil, God's

instructions to people become interpreted as words for knowing what to do and how to act. This is an Old Covenant dynamic of hearing God. The New Covenant is all about knowing God and in knowing God we come to understand who we are in Him and with Him in our lives. This is the kind of relationship God has always wanted with mankind. Hearing God then becomes a substance that empowers us to live. God wants us to hear Him so that we can know Him. He wants us to know Him so that we can know who we really are in life. When we know who we are, we will know what to do. It is an attribute of a changed heart and mind, not one of law and rules.

Hearing God is like carving a statue of an elephant. If you want to carve a statue of an elephant you first need to find a block of wood, stone, or some material the size of the elephant you want to carve. Once you have the piece of material, you simply cut away everything that doesn't look like an elephant. That sounds crazy, but hearing God is like that. God knows who we are and He knows how we hear. He is speaking to us all the time. We hear Him very well. The problem is that we also hear many other things. If we can cut away everything that doesn't sound like God we will end up hearing God very clearly in our lives. The secret to hearing God is found in personally knowing God. If we know who He is and what He is like we will begin to hear Him clearly in our lives. It isn't that He starts talking when we know Him, it is that we finally recognize His voice when we know what His voice sounds like.

God's voice is like radio transmissions or video transmissions in the room. There are hundreds of frequencies transmitting audio and video signals into the air. We don't have to hear them or see them for them to be real. They are real, but we aren't aware of them. It is only when we get a proper receiver for the signals we are seeking to hear or see that we find them. If we have a radio receiver we can tune into radio signals. If we have a television we can tune into television signals. If we have an internet receiver and a computer we can begin to tune into internet signals. The same is true with the voice of God. God is speaking, but we must be listening. God doesn't speak to our natural ears; He speaks to human hearts. The human heart is the receiver for the voice of God. We must learn to hear God in our hearts. This is the place of the human spirit. We must learn to hear God by His Spirit to our spirit. It is then that we can begin to translate the signals of His voice to our souls. Hearing God's voice is all about properly positioning our hearts to hear Him. Hearing God empowers us to live from our hearts and not from our minds.

I have known God for more than forty-two years. The most important thing that I have learned in all of my years in relationship with God is that He is my friend! When I know He is my friend I can hear Him more clearly. He is not angry with me and He isn't seeking to condemn me. He didn't even seek to condemn me when I was a sinner, but sent His only Son to save me! He is not ashamed of me. He wants me to know Him and to know that He is my friend.

The second thing that I have learned about God is that He wants to communicate with people. His thoughts for us are more than can be numbered. His thoughts for us are more than the sand. These are not thoughts of judgment. They are not thoughts of what is right and what is wrong in our lives. They are thoughts of love towards us that offer us hope and a future. They are thoughts that empower us to change in our ways to become like Him in our lives. They will affect the things that are wrong in our lives and turn them toward what is right, but this is the fruit of hearing God's voice and not the purpose for hearing God's voice.

Psalms 40:5 Many, O Lord my God, are Your wonderful works which You have done; and Your thoughts toward us cannot be recounted to You in order; if I would declare and speak of them, they are more than can be numbered.

Psalms 139:17-18 How precious also are Your thoughts to me, O God! How great is the sum of them! If I should count them, they would be more in number than the sand; when I awake, I am still with You.

God's thoughts towards us are not just numerous. His thoughts are precious. They are 'one of a kind' thoughts. Our value to God is that of being a 'one and only' child of God. This is the price that He paid to redeem every human life: He gave His only begotten Son for each and everyone. God sees us in the same way that a father or mother knows that each of their children are unique and precious. His thoughts for us are precious thoughts. He never stops thinking precious thoughts for each and everyone of us. When we are sleeping and not aware of Him, He is still thinking about us. We are a focus of His heart and He wants us to hear His voice. We can assume that He is speaking, but we often approach Him as though we think He has nothing to say. We assume that He only wants to talk to us when He wants to tell us what to do or how to change. What if He just wants to talk to His children? What if He just wants to be our friend? He will tell us what to do when we need to be told, but I think He hopes we will become like Him and know what to do when we need to do it. I think He wants us to do what we see Him doing and we should not expect to be told what to do and how to act every day of our lives.

God is speaking, but we must be listening. If we are not seeking to hear Him we will miss many of the precious thoughts that He has for us. If we don't believe that He is speaking to us we will not open our hearts to hear Him. A radio must 'dial in' to the frequency of a radio station to hear the type of broadcast it is transmitting. We must tune in to God's voice in order to hear the expressions of His voice in our lives.

Psalms 95:7-8 For He is our God, and we are the people of His pasture, and the sheep of His hand. Today, if you will hear His voice: "Do not harden your hearts, as in the rebellion, as in the day of trial in the wilderness..."

It is possible for us to harden our hearts and not hear His voice. God doesn't stop speaking; we simply stop hearing. The children of Israel hardened their hearts toward God because they were more concerned with their own ways than knowing the ways of God. They saw the acts of God, but they did not desire to know what God was like in His character, nature, or way. Moses knew the ways of God, but the children of Israel only saw the acts of God, thus they could not hear Him and live with faith towards Him (Ps. 103:7). Hearing God is the recognition of His voice. It doesn't happen when He speaks, it happens when we hear. God is always speaking. He is always communicating with people, but people must position themselves to hear Him in their hearts.

Hearing God is not about knowing what to do in life. Hearing God is about knowing God. The Old Covenant was an informative one, while the New Covenant is a covenant of transformation. It involves a testimony of changed lives through a personal and intimate relationship with God in Christ.

Life is a journey. It is not merely a path that leads to a final destination. It is a process of living life in a relationship with God that leads to a transition of glory and to knowing God more fully in the life to come. We have each been given a life to live and the point of that life is to know God in all things. Life is not fair. It is very often crazy. Some people have it seemingly easy, while others appear to walk a more difficult path. It is not wise to compare our lives with the lives of others. The point of each man's or woman's journey is to know a personal relationship with God in all things. Let's consider Jesus' story of the two men who built homes.

Matthew 7:24-27 "Therefore whoever hears these sayings of Mine, and does them, I will liken him to a wise man who built his house on the rock: and the rain descended, the floods came, and the winds blew and beat on that house; and it did not fall, for it was founded on the rock. But everyone who hears these sayings of Mine, and does not do them, will be like a foolish man who built his house on the sand: and the rain descended, the floods came, and the winds blew and beat on that house; and it fell. And great was its fall."

In this story there were two men who built houses. They may have had the same architect. The blue prints for the homes may have been exactly the same. The number of rooms may have been exactly the same. The materials for building each house may have even been the same.

They could have chosen the same interior and exterior decorations. These houses may have been built in the exact same geographical location. The difference was in the foundation of each house. One man dug down to the rock, while the other man simply built his house on the surface of the sand.

Jesus explained the process of digging. Both individuals heard God, but only one man responded to God's voice. One man listened to what God said, while the other man simply focused on building his house. I believe that the rock in the story is Christ. The point of hearing God was not so either man would know how to build their house. The point of hearing God was so that each one would know God. One realized that hearing and responding to God was all about a close relationship with God. It was about being connected to the rock. The other man heard God and simply thought life was about his own desires, dreams, vision, purpose, tasks, creativity, expressions, and any other thing that is a part of the house called one's life. The man who built his house on the rock knew that life was about always knowing the presence of God in the foundation of all things.

In both cases, the rain fell, floods came, and winds blew and beat hard against each house. Life is not about avoiding circumstances. It is about knowing God in all things. The one who knew God's presence withstood everything that he faced in life, while the one who simply heard God and built his house suffered the great loss of things. Do we love the One who is the foundation of our lives or do we love the purpose of our lives? Our purpose in life is nothing without the presence of Christ. We are expressions of Him and to be expressions of Him we must depend upon Him in all things. He is not just a voice within. He is Christ within! Our lives are dependent upon knowing Him in all things. Do we know that all things will work together because He is always with us? King David knew that no matter where he found himself, God would be there. Was it because God lives everywhere? David said that if he went to the realm of the dead (hell), God would be there. Does God live in the realm of the dead? If He did, could we call it the realm of the dead? Did David believe that God was everywhere or did he simply know that God would never leave him? Where could he go and not find God, for God was the foundation of His life and God would never leave him. God wanted to know David and David wanted to know God. It was a love relationship, not a means to knowing what to do in life. It was about friendship with God and man, not about an anointing from heaven for an earthly plan.

Psalms 139:1-6 O LORD, You have searched me and known me. You know my sitting down and my rising up; You understand my thought afar off. You comprehend my path and my lying down, and are acquainted with all my ways. For there is not a word on my tongue, but behold, O LORD, You know it altogether. You have hedged me behind and before, and laid Your hand upon me. Such knowledge is too wonderful for me; it is high, I cannot attain it.

David understood that God wanted a relationship with Him. The first important thing of life is that God knows you and He wants to know you. He wants you to know Him too.

David knew that because God loved Him, He would never leave Him. God was always present in His life. Like the rock in the foundation of the house, Christ is the foundation of every human life and destiny.

Psalms 139:7-10 Where can I go from Your Spirit? Or where can I flee from Your presence? If I ascend into heaven, You are there; if I make my bed in hell, behold, You are there. If I take the wings of the morning, and dwell in the uttermost parts of the sea, even there Your hand shall lead me, and Your right hand shall hold me.

I don't believe that David was pointing out the sovereignty of God. He was pointing to the imminence and intimacy of God. God was faithful to David and God would never leave Him. There is no place that David could go that God would not go too. There is no place in your life where you can go that God will not go too!

Consider the rest of Psalms 139, but consider it from the view of knowing God as the Rock of your life. Hearing Him is not always about knowing what to do, but it is always about knowing Him. Let Him love you and He will empower your love for Him!

Chapter 1

Foundations For Hearing God

1. Hearing God is Connected to Who You Are

Hearing God is directly connected to knowing who we are in Christ. Before Jesus entered into His ministry as Christ in the earth, He heard the voice of His Father in regard to who He was. God didn't tell Him what to do. He told Him, and those around Him, who He was.

Matthew 3:16-17 When He had been baptized, Jesus came up immediately from the water; and behold, the heavens were opened to Him, and He saw the Spirit of God descending like a dove and alighting upon Him. And suddenly a voice came from heaven, saying, "This is My beloved Son, in whom I am well pleased."

Jesus hadn't done any miracles, preached any sermons, cast out any devils, multiplied any bread, or raised anyone from the dead and God, His Father, was 'pleased with Him'. The basis of Jesus hearing the voice of God was one of identity, not one of instruction or command. Jesus knew who He was and He also knew who His Father was.

When the devil challenged Jesus in the wilderness, he didn't challenge Him in His ability. He challenged Him in His identity.

Matthew 4:3 Now when the tempter came to Him, he said, "If You are the Son of God, command that these stones become bread."

It was in knowing He was the Son of God that Jesus could recognize that the voice speaking to Him was not the voice of His heavenly Father. He knew that the voice of God is not about knowing what to do or the ability to do anything. He knew that the voice of God makes man come alive. When Jesus said, "It is written," I believe He was talking about His own heart and mind. I don't believe He was quoting Deuteronomy; Deuteronomy was a shadow quotation of Him. The Scriptures testified of Him, not He of Scripture (Jn. 5:39). Jesus was a New Covenant man in an Old Covenant time and it was the testimony of the New Covenant that caused Him to be who He was. The law of God was written upon His own heart and mind, because He found His life in a personal relationship with God as His Father (Jer. 31:31-34).

Matthew 4:4 But He answered and said, "It is written, 'Man shall not live by bread alone, but by every word that proceeds from the mouth of God.' "

I don't think that the devil came to Jesus and told Him he was the devil. He is a deceiver and in the same way we are tempted, Jesus was tempted. Jesus discerned that the voice speaking to Him was not the voice of His heavenly Father. Jesus knew that the words of God bring life, and the words of the tempter did not bring life to His heart. This truth is revealed in the continued temptation presented to Jesus by the devil in the wilderness. In a second attempt to deceive Jesus, the devil quoted the book, but the book is not the key to human victory. The voice that inspired the book and inspires the hearts of men was the key to human triumph.

Matthew 4:5-7 Then the devil took Him up into the holy city, set Him on the pinnacle of the temple, and said to Him, "If You are the Son of God, throw Yourself down. For it is written: 'He shall give His angels charge over you,' and, 'In their hands they shall bear you up, lest you dash your foot against a stone.' " Jesus said to him, "It is written again, 'You shall not tempt the LORD your God.' "

The devil was quoting the book of Psalms to Jesus, but Jesus recognized that the words were not the words of His Father. Although they were Scripturally correct, they were not true to the character of God. Jesus' response was again one of revealing that the word of God was written in His own heart and mind and that the words of God in the mouth of the devil are still the words of the devil. Although the words of Jesus are words in the book of Deuteronomy, I believe they were the testimony of His own heart and mind. Again, Deuteronomy testified of Jesus, not Jesus of Deuteronomy.

The devil's third attempt to deceive Jesus involved Jesus's purpose as a man. Jesus was destined to redeem the nations of men, but the devil tempted him to take the nations for Himself. Jesus knew that the redemption of humanity would be worship to His heavenly Father, but the devil promised Him the nations if He would but worship him. Jesus knew that the voice of God does not serve any self-purpose, but rather it empowers everyone to live for the well-being of God and others.

Matthew 4:8-10 Again, the devil took Him up on an exceedingly high mountain, and showed Him all the kingdoms of the world and their glory. And he said to Him, "All these things I will give You if You will fall down and worship me." Then Jesus said to him, "Away with you, Satan! For it is written, 'You shall worship the LORD your God, and Him only you shall serve.'"

Hearing God is not about receiving words from God that make us great or able to accomplish great things in life. Hearing God is about knowing how great God is and how great it is to be His son or daughter. If we have a healthy, and secure, relationship with God we will hear Him more clearly. We don't need to earn God's love, so hearing God won't make God love us more. It will simply make us more aware of His love. God is our Father and He loves us as His children. We don't hear God so He will be pleased with us. We know He is pleased with us and that empowers us to hear Him clearly. We live to please Him, because we know how pleased He is with us as His children. We are pleased to love Him and hearing Him is staying connected to His heart in all things.

2. His Voice Removes All Shame

God wants us to hear Him. One of the greatest hindrances to hearing God's voice is shame. When we carry shame we are not open to hearing God clearly. When Adam fell to sin, the first thing he and Eve did was to seek to cover up their nakedness. When they heard God walking in the garden they hid from Him for the shame of their sin (Gen. 3:7-8). God came looking for them, as it seemed to be a usual act of God to walk with them in the cool of the day (Gen. 3:9). Adam and Eve covered themselves with the leaves of the trees, but God made them tunics of skin and clothed them (Gen. 3:21). He covered them with a testimony of a sacrifice for their sin. His aim was not to condemn them, but to cover them. In the testimony of the required offerings, the first offering was a burnt offering. It was an offering of blood, the life of the flesh. That offering was given in order for man to have access to the presence of God. It was a testimony for the forgiveness of sin so they could be clear to hear God in a relationship with Him. This sacrifice of shed blood was a testimony of removing shame from the hearts of men, not one of putting shame upon them. The blood of Jesus Christ has brought us near to God (Eph. 2:13), a testimony of removing shame from our lives so we can have a relationship with God, hearing His voice. God's words to us are words that remove the shame in our lives. They are not words that condemn us in our shame. They are words that invite us to His presence through the forgiveness of our sins.

When we choose to live with shameful ways, or among shameful things, it isn't God that condemns us. It is the shameful things that condemn us. Those things will hinder us from hearing God who wants to speak to us freely. God wants us all to know His voice and the testimony of His love, but shameful things will cause us to hide from Him and we will not hear His voice. When we do hear His voice we often twist His words to justify our shameful ways. This keeps us bound to the feelings of guilt and condemnation that are not found in a relationship with God.

One day Jesus met a Samaritan woman in the city of Sychar. As He stood by the well of Jacob, a Samaritan woman came to draw water. It was in a time and culture where women were considered to be less valuable than men. Jews looked down upon Samaritans as being an inferior race of compromise. No doubt this woman was living under the heaviness of her culture and society. Her eyes were likely all you could see for the covering of her head. Jesus spoke to her and asked her to give Him a drink. She was probably shocked that a Jewish man would speak to her. Her answer was one of dismay that a Jewish man would speak to her. I am sure she felt the cultural pressure of the day that invoked her to embrace a preconceived feeling of shame being placed upon her. Her response to Jesus was one of asking why He would ask her for a drink since He was a Jew and she was a Samaritan.

John 4:9 Then the woman of Samaria said to Him, "How is it that You, being a Jew, ask a drink from me, a Samaritan woman?" For Jews have no dealings with Samaritans.

If Jesus were an Old Covenant prophet, He would have probably said something like this: "Woman, the Spirit of God shows me that you are a sinner. You are living with a man who is not your husband and you must repent, that you might make things right with God. Change your ways and God will reveal Himself to you. You must repent of your sin that you might seek Him and find Him." Jesus didn't say that! It seems that God wasn't looking for the woman to find Him; He had simply come to tell her that He had found her. She had been looking for love in all the wrong places and today He had come to show Her that He loved her. He wanted to give her life-giving water that would satisfy her soul.

John 4:10-14 Jesus answered and said to her, "If you knew the gift of God, and who it is who says to you, 'Give Me a drink,' you would have asked Him, and He would have given you living water." The woman said to Him, "Sir, You have nothing to draw with, and the well is deep. Where then do You get that living water? Are You greater than our father Jacob, who gave us the well, and drank from it himself, as well as his sons and his livestock?" Jesus answered and said to her, "Whoever drinks of this water will thirst again, but whoever drinks of the water that I shall give him will never thirst. But the water that I shall give him will become in him a fountain of water springing up into everlasting life."

God simply wanted to give the woman life. That life was for her to know Jesus and God her Father. He wasn't there to say shame on her; He was there to take shame off of her so she could recognize the voice of God in her life. Her heart longed for the life that Jesus spoke of. She was likely tired of the same repeated environment of bondage and shame day after day in her life. The drudgery of repeating each day was weighing heavy upon her.

John 4:15 The woman said to Him, "Sir, give me this water, that I may not thirst, nor come here to draw."

Jesus's response to her was an act of giving her the life that she asked for. He knew that the man she was with was not her husband. He knew that she had previously been with five other men. I believe that His statement to her was one that freed her from the condemnation of her sin. It was a statement to remove the shame from her life.

John 4:16 Jesus said to her, "Go, call your husband, and come here." The woman answered and said, "I have no husband." Jesus said to her, "You have well said, 'I have no husband,' for you have had five husbands, and the one whom you now have is not your husband; in that you spoke truly."

The words of Jesus revealed that the woman had been looking for love in all the wrong places. She had five major disappointments and now the man she was with had no idea who she really was. She had been treated as someone of little value in her culture and in her relationships, but Jesus had come to reveal to her who she really was. She was born to be loved by God!

The woman was so blessed she forgot why she had come to the well. She left her waterpot and went to the city to tell everyone about what had happened. She had met a man who gave her life and not bondage and shame. She could hear God, because God had revealed to her that there was no shame upon her life that could keep His love from being revealed to her.

I believe that a key to hearing God's voice is to let God remove the things of shame in our lives. God's voice doesn't condemn us in our sin; it frees us from sin. God's voice is heard when there is a revelation of God's love!

3. Hearing God Brings Faith

Hearing God results in faith in our hearts. Faith is a natural result of a supernatural relationship with God. Maybe it is more accurate to say that faith is a natural result of a relationship with God, who is supernatural in every way. Faith works through love. When we love someone we hear what he or she says to us. It is very easy to misunderstand someone we don't love. It is easy to twist the words of those we judge and end up bringing destruction to the relationship and even destruction to our own lives in some way.

The apostle Peter wrote some difficult words to understand when addressing the topic of a new heaven and a new earth. He was addressing a relevant issue at the time, for a scattered Jewish church that was facing persecution in the process of birthing a firstfruit New Covenant temple that was forcing the end of the Old Covenant structure, system, and administration. Peter cautioned that Paul also wrote some difficult things to understand and that people who are unstable and untaught end up twisting the writings of Paul to their own destruction.

2 Peter 3:14-16 Therefore, beloved, looking forward to these things, be diligent to be found by Him in peace, without spot and blameless; and consider that the longsuffering of our Lord is salvation—as also our beloved brother Paul, according to the wisdom given to him, has written to you, as also in all his epistles, speaking in them of these things, in which are some things hard to understand, which

*untaught and unstable people twist to their own destruction, as they
do also the rest of the Scriptures.*

What does it mean to be unstable? I believe that stability has to do with
relationships. When we take an offense with someone, we often make
a judgment of him or her. Our understanding then becomes darkened
and we become self-focused, self-preserving, or self-defensive in some
way. We become defiled in our relationship towards them. When this
happens, it doesn't matter what they say. We have entered into instability
in our relationship towards them and we will not hear what they say to
us correctly. We must seek to be stable in our relationship with God and
with those who love us or we will become hindered in our ability to hear
God. If we carry an offense, a judgment, or defilement in some way, we
will twist what God says in a destructive manner.

What does it mean to be untaught? Many times I hear people
complain about the way the Bible is written and even about the way
that God talks to them. They grumble, questioning why God doesn't
speak clearly. Why is the Bible written in a way that it is difficult to
understand at times? Why doesn't God just tell us things clearly? Part
of our problem is that we expect God to plainly tell us what to do or
how to act. God wants us to know Him more than to know what to do
or how to act. He wants us to understand His heart. King Solomon said
that it is the glory of God to hide things and the glory of kings to search
those things out (Pr. 25:2). He could have written it this way: 'It is the
glory of God to hide things and peasants never discover a thing!' God
knows that we have the ability to be kings; therefore, He speaks in a
way that requires us to dig. The secret things belong to God, but when
they are revealed to us they belong to us and to our children forever
(Deut. 29:29). We must learn God's language in order to understand
Him. Hearing God is like a radio tuning into the frequency of radio
transmissions. It is like a television tuning into video frequencies. We
must have the correct receiver and we must know what frequency to
tune into. We hear God with our hearts, but the frequency we must
tune our hearts to is found in the character, nature, way, power, and
authority of God's heart. We must learn what God sounds like. We must

learn what He means in the language of His heart. If we were going to be a missionary to China we would need to find someone in China who knows the language and the culture of the people of China. We would need a helper, a translator, and a teacher in regard to the ways and culture of the Chinese people. We cannot expect to be effective in hearing or relating to the Chinese people if our thinking is bound to a Western mindset. We must learn the culture and language of those we need to hear. The same is true with God. In order to understand God, we must learn His language. We must learn His ways. We must learn the culture of heaven in order to hear the One who speaks to us from heaven. He wants to make us like Him and He isn't willing to compromise who He truly is. The good news is, we have a Helper, a Translator, and a Teacher in regard to the ways and the culture of God. We have the Holy Spirit and we have the words of His inspiration in the form of the Scriptures. We don't study the Scripture so we will know what to do. We invite the Holy Spirit to help us understand the heart of God when reading the Scriptures. The Scripture is filled with symbols, phrases, words, and expressions that help us understand the character, nature, way, power, and authority of God. The Scripture is filled with principles, patterns, and values that help us to recognize the voice of God and understand His words to our hearts. We must be taught in the language and culture of God to understand Him when He speaks. If we think He is angry and mean we will misunderstand the words that are supposed to reveal who He is. If we view Him as a judge and not a Father, we will misinterpret His decisions. We must know Him and we must know His heart.

We must be stable and taught to understand what God is saying to us in our lives. God is speaking, but we must learn to tune into the frequency of His voice. We hear Him through our hearts, but His voice is only heard clearly through an understanding of His heart. We must seek to be stable and taught to properly understand the voice of God in our lives.

4. God's Words Are Life-Giving Words

How do we recognize the voice of God? How can we recognize His words to us? We hear God clearly; the problem is that we also hear many other things. If we can learn to reject the words that are not from God, we can clearly recognize the words that are from Him. God's words are life-giving words. When He speaks to our hearts, we come alive from within. It is not a false life that promotes pride or any stubbornness of the flesh. It is a voice that springs to life from within us. We know they are life-giving words because they inspire us to give life to others. Jesus said that if the thirsty come to Him they won't just receive refreshing words for themselves. He said that there would be a release of life-giving words through them to others. When God speaks it inspires life in every way!

John 7:37-38 On the last day, that great day of the feast, Jesus stood and cried out, saying, "If anyone thirsts, let him come to Me and drink. He who believes in Me, as the Scripture has said, out of his heart will flow rivers of living water."

Living water is an expression of life that makes us come alive. Living water that flows from our hearts is an expression of life that brings life to others. Hearing God doesn't merely serve to satisfy the needs of our hearts. Hearing God activates the purpose of our hearts. We were born to bring life to this world. We were born to bring life to others. When we hear God it activates the testimony of life within us. It empowers us to be expressions of God's life to the world. This is a testimony of hearing God.

Hearing God releases life-giving expressions from our hearts. Hearing God happens when we come to God. When we are close to Him we hear Him. When we hear Him His life-giving words become a river of life to others. If what we hear doesn't inspire life to others, it was not the voice of God. Life inspiring words are a testimony of the tree of life and they are not rooted in the tree of the knowledge of good and evil. They don't inspire judgments of right and wrong. God's voice doesn't inspire judgments of good and evil. It releases an anointing that feeds the hungry and heals what is sick. It is a life-giving flow that breaks every curse and produces the fruit of life.

Revelation 22:1-5 And he showed me a pure river of water of life, clear as crystal, proceeding from the throne of God and of the Lamb. In the middle of its street, and on either side of the river, was the tree of life, which bore twelve fruits, each tree yielding its fruit every month. The leaves of the tree were for the healing of the nations. And there shall be no more curse, but the throne of God and of the Lamb shall be in it, and His servants shall serve Him. They shall see His face, and His name shall be on their foreheads. There shall be no night there: They need no lamp nor light of the sun, for the Lord God gives them light. And they shall reign forever and ever.

The river that flows from our hearts is like a street. It is a flow of life that serves the purpose of the destiny of life in the earth. It is connected to all that God has said yesterday and continues in all that God is in the future of our lives. Every thought, attitude, focus, dream, vision, action, and word from God flows through the tree of life before it touches the lives of others. Like the planting of trees, it is generational in its potency. It brings life to the generations of men and women in the earth. The fruit of God's voice brings life to the hungry. The touch of God's voice heals all that is sick. The voice of God reveals the blessings of God, the presence of God, the forgiveness of God, and the fullness of His purpose to and through our lives to others. God's voice empowers us to see His face. Shame is gone, forgiveness has come, and His love is a revelation in our hearts. The voice of God gives us hope for the future and destroys the fear of night. It brings the light of God's grace into our hearts and an overcoming power to reign in life. God's voice may not get us out of our present circumstances, but it will for sure reveal that God is with us in every aspect of our lives. God's words are life-giving words. This is how we know the voice of God.

5. God's Words Produce Faith

God's words produce faith. Faith happens when we hear Him. Faith is always towards someone, it comes from hearing them. Faith toward God comes by hearing God (Rom. 10:17). We must stay in the place where faith happens in order to be obedient to the faith. Faith toward

God is not merely having faith toward a promise He has given us. There is a certain glory in standing to see a promise fulfilled, but New Covenant faith is much more. Faith produces actions that demonstrate love and love is always towards a person, not a promise. Faith towards a promise alone is idolatry.

Faith only happens in the place of hearing God. If we heard God a week ago and we are trying to remain faithful to what God said, we have already walked a week into a covenant of law. We must stay in a face-to-face relationship with God to remain in the place of faith. Faith is not the testimony of having heard God yesterday. It is the testimony of hearing God now and continually hearing Him into tomorrow. Hearing God is a faith-inspiring place! Staying in the place of hearing God will make us faithful to Him. We will be full of faith when we remain in the place where faith happens. There can never be a gap between God and us. There can never be a separation in our relationship with Him. We must stay in the place where we can hear His voice.

Faith is not a belief system. It is the substance that inspires actions towards God when we hear Him in our hearts. Faith comes by hearing God speak. A revelation of love for God allows us to hear and understand His words in our hearts. The result is seen in faith inspired actions towards Him. Faith is not towards something. Faith is towards a person. When I have a revelation of love for my wife it allows me to hear her. I hear what she says and it inspires me to act in her direction. This is the source of faithfulness in our relationship. It is not an obligation towards accountability. It is part of the dance of relationship in my love for her. Hearing her inspires me to do actions from my heart for her. This is even truer in my relationship with God, but the principle is the same.

The opposite of faith is natural sight. We walk by faith and not by sight (2 Cor. 5:7). That sight is natural sight. It is how something looks naturally. It may be how I think it appears to be. It could be how I think it sounds, how it makes me feel, how I expect it to turn out, or even how circumstances of my past have affected my ability to see things in the present. Natural sight is dependent upon how things are, look, sound, feel, appear to be, or are presumed to be. It can be true naturally, or perceived to be true naturally. Many people think that the opposite of faith is fear, but fear is simply the environment that keeps us bound to natural sight. Love is the environment that spawns faith. Perfect love casts out all fear and where perfect love is there is a clear environment for faith to be conceived. Faith inspires actions of love. Fear inspires actions of insecurity. Faith actions seek to give life to others, while actions of fear seek to take life from them. Getting my needs met is a fear-based mentality and it is not the environment that produces faith. Giving life to others is a love inspired mentality and it is the environment that spawns faith.

When we hear God it will inspire faith, and that faith will be seen in actions of love towards Him and towards others. This is the evidence of faith in our hearts. Faith produces faithfulness! Faithfulness is not an act of mere obedience. It is a faith-inspired attitude that produces faith-inspired actions. Faith is always towards someone, it comes from hearing him or her. Faith towards God comes from hearing God. Faithfulness comes from staying in the place of hearing someone. Staying in the place of hearing God makes you faithful to Him. It is the place where faith can fill your heart.

As believers in Christ, we are to be obedient to the faith. This is not an obligation. This is a supernatural inspiration that flows from the environment of love within our hearts. Faithfulness cannot be an obligation. It must be an inspiration. It cannot be something that you hold yourself to. It must be a revelation that holds you. Faithfulness is an attribute of the heart, not a discipline of the mind. Faithfulness is empowered by grace, not by law. It is a testimony of truth, not a constraint of conscience. This is the testimony of being obedient to the faith. Living in faith will be seen in our acts of love toward God and others. This is a witness of God's voice in our lives.

6. God's Words are Kingdom Words

God's words are ones that reveal the life and blessings of His kingdom. God's kingdom is not something we observe in the signs around us. It is a kingdom that we come to know from within our hearts. It is an inside-of-us kingdom that then transforms the outward expressions of our lives to the kingdoms of this world. The kingdoms of the world do not determine the kingdom of God, but the kingdom of God determines the future of the kingdoms around us. He who is in us is greater than he who is in the world. When God speaks to us it activates the testimony of Christ's kingdom within our hearts.

Luke 17:20-21 Now when He was asked by the Pharisees when the kingdom of God would come, He answered them and said, "The kingdom of God does not come with observation; nor will they say, "See here!' or 'See there!' For indeed, the kingdom of God is within you."

The kingdom of God within our hearts is a kingdom of righteousness, peace, and joy in the Holy Spirit (Rom. 14:17). When God speaks to us it activates, facilitates, and releases the power of true righteousness, peace, and joy in the Holy Spirit within our hearts. I believe that true righteousness is a total dependency upon God from within our hearts. It is not merely the act of doing right things. It is the testimony of a right relationship with God that in turn produces a right relationship with people. Righteousness is not the result of an action in our lives, but it will bear the fruit of actions that exhibit a love for God and a love for others. I believe that righteousness is the cry from our hearts that confesses that God is our God. It is not seen as a lip service to Him, but it is found as a life-giving ambiance and atmosphere in our hearts that says God is our God and Jesus is Lord. When God speaks to us it activates the substance of that passion within our hearts. The supernatural presence of God's righteousness in our hearts will empower us to be God-seekers and no longer seekers of our own carnal desires.

When God speaks it activates the substance of peace in the Holy Spirit within us. Peace is not the absence of conflict. It is a place of having no gap between God and us. There is no separation between God's love and us. The empowerment of God's presence in our lives reveals a testimony of God in our lives that becomes evident to those around us. When God's peace is in our lives we bear a testimony of being God's people. Something begins to come off of our lives that testifies we are one with God. We are God's people. God's peace within our hearts will even empower us to forsake the things that seek to draw as away from His love. The supernatural presence of God's peace will transform our hearts to become people who spill over with a testimony of His grace.

When God speaks it also activates the substance of joy in the Holy Spirit within us. It is the fruit of an understanding of God's manifest presence within us. We and God live together. In the presence of God there is the fullness of joy (Ps. 16:11). The voice of God releases the joy of knowing God as our Father from within our hearts. We discover the joy of living for Him and with Him. It is not some mystery that happens in the world around us. It is an often-inexpressible joy of life from within our hearts in knowing that we are His family and we live together. The supernatural presence of God's joy in our hearts empowers us to be His family of life in the world and to the world around us.

When God speaks it activates these attributes of the kingdom of God within our hearts. We become God-seekers, testifiers of God, and revelations of His inheritance through our lives. God speaks to the human heart from within and it is the frequency of His heart that confirms His voice within. We must keep our hearts open and listen for the sound that activates us to know that God is our God, we are His people, and we live together.

God's words to us are words of authority and not merely words of power. They are life-giving and they do not motivate responses that inspire us to grasp for power. His words cause us to desire to give life to others. They are supernatural words of life that enable us to be givers of life to others in supernatural ways. They are words that reveal God's mercy and grace to and through our lives. They are not condemning words of law, but life-empower words of grace. They reveal that God's mercy is new every day and that His grace can empower us in every way. They confirm in our hearts that we are justified to live by the love of Christ and we are now empowered to live by the love of the same. God's words speak the truth in love and thus they are words that cast out all fear (1Jn. 4:18). Even when inspiring responses of change they are words that reveal God's love in our hearts and not condemnation or shame.

7. Hearing God Gives Us Life

Hearing God is what gives us life. He is our life and we live on every expression that comes from Him. He wants to speak to us and He is in fact speaking to us all of the time. We must tune our hearts to the frequency of His heart to hear Him.

God's words bring a revelation of Jesus Christ and the power of God's grace. Grace is the manifest power of God's Spirit in our lives that changes us. If there is no change, there is no evidence of grace. Grace happens when there is a revelation of Christ in us. When we see Christ in us, grace happens!

1 Peter 1:13-16 Therefore gird up the loins of your mind, be sober, and rest your hope fully upon the grace that is to be brought to you at the revelation of Jesus Christ; as obedient children, not conforming yourselves to the former lusts, as in your ignorance; but as He who called you is holy, you also be holy in all your conduct, because it is written, "Be holy, for I am holy."

When we have a revelation of Jesus Christ in our lives, we are changed. The fruit of His manifested reality in us is a change in our lives. We become like Him when we see Him. Hearing God is all about seeing Him. Hearing God is about knowing God, not merely knowing what to do. God doesn't change our lives by telling us what to do or how to act. Our actions are empowered by a supernatural change in our hearts. When we see Jesus Christ we are changed.

Every revelation from God is an invitation to have an encounter with God, so that God can transform us to become something of a revelation of Him. This is the true testimony of hearing God. Hearing God is a part of the process of Christ's life. Hearing God is part of the fabric of life. It is a testimony of intimacy with God in all things.

God speaks to our hearts and so we must keep our hearts with all diligence in order to hear Him clearly (Pr. 4:23). Our hearts must be spontaneous before God and spontaneous with the life of God to others. They must be deep with a focus toward the things of God and a forsaking and forgetting of the things of the past. Our hearts must be broken with a willingness to yield to the will of God. We must let go of the things that would create bitter roots and strongholds that produce dry places that harbor earthly, sensual, and even demonic influences. Our hearts must be fervent. We must be pure and passionate in our love for God and others. These internal ingredients will inspire our hearts to release the flow of God's life to the world. These are the issues of the heart that keep an open path to hearing the voice of God in our lives. It is within our hearts that we can receive a revelation of Jesus Christ. This is the birthing place of grace in our lives. It is the birthing place of change in our lives. It is the place of knowing God.

Hearing God will guide our lives, but it is not a guidance of information. It is a guidance that comes from the power of God's transformation within us. We become empowered from within in our walk of life. I believe that divine guidance will get us into the future of our lives, but it is more about dancing with God than it is in receiving unsealed orders from Him. We don't just want information from God; we want to walk in the steps given by Him that lead us in a path towards His likeness and image in our lives. Hearing God isn't about knowing what to do. It is about being intimate with God. Our ability to hear God's voice will bring divine guidance into our lives, but that guidance is more for a relationship with Him than it is about making right decisions or knowing what we are doing.

To receive God's guidance in our lives we must first want to receive His guidance. We cannot embrace other forms of guidance and expect to maintain a pure path of direction from Him. We all have other forms of guidance that we must forsake. Some things are obvious while other things are subtle in the way they motivate us in wrong directions. I believe that we all hear God very well, but we also hear many other things. We must learn to cut away the things that are not His voice. When we cut away what is not Him we will be left with His pure voice in our lives. As I have previously stated, it is like carving an elephant. If we want to carve an elephant we get a piece of material the size of the elephant we want and then we cut away everything that doesn't look like an elephant. God's voice is in our lives and we must learn to cut away everything that doesn't sound like God. Therefore, we study His word not to know what to do or how to act; we study His word to know what God is like in His character, nature, way, power, and authority. When we know what He is like as a person, we recognize His voice when He speaks.

Unless we know God in His character and nature we can be susceptible to hearing a wrong voice. We study His written word not to know what to do, but to know Him. We study every expression of Him so that we will know the character, nature, way, power, and authority of who He is. Unless we know God in His character and nature we are apt to hear a wrong voice and believe it is Him.

Chapter 2

Hearing God Will Guide Your Life

1. Hearing God is About Knowing God

Hearing God is not about knowing what to do in life. Hearing God is about knowing God. God wants to guide our lives, but His guidance is not meant to be instructions from His world to our world. His guidance is more like dancing. Our worlds are not separate from His and His world is not separate from ours. His is the Kingdom that consumes all the kingdoms of the world. I lost my life only to find it in Him. I laid my life down to pick it up new as a testimony for His glory. I was born for His glory and I have partnered with God as He leads me in the path of life. It is a supernatural mystery with elegant steps of divine direction. Divine guidance is the dance of life with God revealed through the intimate steps of relationship with Him in all things. God's voice is a testimony to His presence in our lives. The true witness of His voice is revealed through the testimony of Christ in us. We don't want God to give us instructions that simply allow us to know what to do and live lives separate from Him. We want to know Him in all things! His voice is a testimony of His presence in our lives.

1 John 4:1-3 Beloved, do not believe every spirit, but test the spirits, whether they are of God; because many false prophets have gone out into the world. By this you know the Spirit of God: Every spirit that confesses that Jesus Christ has come in the flesh is of God, and every spirit that does not confess that Jesus Christ has come in the flesh is not of God. And this is the spirit of the Antichrist, which you have heard was coming, and is now already in the world.

It is not merely the spirit that says that Jesus came in the flesh as a man two thousand years ago that is the witness of being the Spirit of God. It is the spirit that confesses that Jesus has come in the flesh that is of God. The term 'has come' is in a perfect and imperfect tense, meaning it is both a reality that has happened and also continues to happen. The Greek word in this text does not refer to an event that happened in the past. It refers to a continually happening event. The witness to the voice of God is the Spirit of Christ within the believer. There are three that testify upon the earth and they are the water (Word), the Spirit, and the Blood (1 Jn. 5:8). The Word and the Spirit are a witness to the life of Christ (Blood) within the heart of every believer. When the Word and the Spirit come together in our hearts it activates the testimony of Christ within our lives.

Divine guidance is hearing God's voice and responding to what He says. It can include knowing what to do in life, but it is more about responding to Him in a relationship with Him in life. When God speaks it inspires us to love Him and to love others. The true prophetic Spirit of Christ is filled with love and it empowers us to love our neighbors and to love ourselves.

Divine guidance is the fruit of a relationship with God in our hearts. It is not complicated; however, other things influence our lives and can make divine guidance complicated. Experiences in life affect our emotions and often cause us to have impure motives. We make judgments in our hearts and then we become prejudice in our thought processes. We can become bound to habits and thought patterns, and even exhibit actions that restrain and restrict our ability to properly interpret God's voice when He speaks to us. We may hear God perfectly, but our emotions, motives, prejudices, habit patterns, thoughts, and actions influence us to misunderstand what God says to us. These things can prevent us from hearing God, or cause us to twist what God is saying and become bound to deceptions that lead us away from what God intends for us.

Our own natural understandings will resist the voice of God in our lives. The opposite of faith is natural sight and God's voice is a voice of faith (2 Cor. 5:7). When someone hurts us in some way we tend to believe lies about other people. When someone hurts us we buy into a lie that people cannot be trusted. When this happens, God will sometimes use a person or a voice that will remind us of what we cannot trust. God wants to heal our hearts more than merely tell us what to do. God is not trying to trick us; He simply wants to heal our hearts. He doesn't merely want us to be servants or slaves to His will. He wants us to be His children who know and partake in His character, nature, and way. When He guides our lives He has more in mind than simply helping us make decisions in life.

Guidance doesn't just happen. It is not just instantly understood. The voice of God is automatically heard through a relationship with God, but understanding His voice is a process. Although His voice is automatically heard through a relationship with Him, we don't always recognize what He is saying. We know He is speaking, but we misinterpret the words.

Beyond hearing Him is learning to allow Him to guide our lives. It is like learning to dance. We must learn to hear and respond to His voice. It is not a set of methods, but it includes steps that could be interpreted as methods. Guidance is not about methods that lead to right actions, it is steps from, and for, a right relationship with Him. Divine guidance is a very personal thing in each of our lives. Learning the skill of divine guidance begins with a desire to receive His instruction. That desire for His instruction is something that we must ask for. We must also learn to embrace His instructions in our lives. This includes seeking out others who can help us learn the skill of dancing the dance of guidance with God.

Hebrews 13:7 Remember those who rule over you, who have spoken the word of God to you, whose faith follow, considering the outcome of their conduct.

Remembering those whom God has given to assist us in life is not just remembering who they are. It involves seeking them out so that we know what is in them. We are to seek out those whom God has placed in our lives and we are to look to see the dance of God's guidance in their lives, so that we can be inspired in our own relational journey with God. The fruit of their lives is a testimony that we might find our own relationship with God which bears the fruit of life that others can also see.

When it comes to divine guidance I believe that God is extremely intimate and personal. He wants to speak to us on a specific and personal level, but He is also willing to guide our steps in a providential way. His providence is not based upon the strength of His control, but rather upon the intimacy of His heart. When we commit our way to Him, and trust Him with all of our hearts, He is willing to give us His desires and guide our steps even when we do not realize He is guiding us.

Psalms 37:3-6 Trust in the LORD, and do good; dwell in the land, and feed on His faithfulness. Delight yourself also in the LORD, and He shall give you the desires of your heart. Commit your way to the LORD, trust also in Him, and He shall bring it to pass. He shall bring forth your righteousness as the light, and your justice as the noonday.

The psalmist's words are not ones of dependence upon a sovereign God, but those of someone who depends upon the love of God. It is the faithfulness of a loving Father that guides our hearts and our steps in life. It is not merely the providence of a powerful God.

Psalms 37:23-24 The steps of a good man are ordered by the LORD, and He delights in his way. Though he fall, he shall not be utterly cast down; for the LORD upholds him with His hand.

It is out of a relationship with God that He will guide our steps. He delights in the course of life of those who love Him and commit their lives to walking in His ways. Even if that man or woman should fall, God will pick them up and help them.

Many people profess that God is in control, but I believe that God is in charge and man is in control. Perhaps the semantics of words may warrant us to say that God is in control and man is in charge, but the fact is that God gave man dominion over the works of His hands (Ps. 8). It is important that men and women get intimate with God who is in charge, so that they may exercise life-giving actions in all they are in control of. I believe that God gets blamed for many things based upon a paradigm of thinking that puts the greatest emphasis on God being sovereign, and not enough upon Him being intimate. If I am in control of selling cars on a car lot and I am a liar and a cheat I will make the owner of the car dealership look very bad. Even if the owner is a fair and good man my cheating ways will defame the character of the one who is truly in charge. I must be intimate with the one in charge in order to represent him in all that I am in control of. If I fail in being a good representative of the one in charge I cannot blame the one in charge for my failures. It is my failure for not being in a right relationship with the one in charge that caused me to misrepresent him in my dealings.

It is the will of the human heart that determines God's providential and specific guidance for men. When we seek Him we find Him. When we call on Him, He is quick to answer. What is it that makes God, God? Is it His sovereignty? The Greeks had many gods and therefore the Christian God could only be incorporated into their thinking if He out-trumped all of the other gods. By this criteria, to be God He must be omnipotent, omniscient, and omnipresent.

Is God omnipotent? I believe that He can be, but He chooses not to be as often as He can. He said that the traditions of men make His word of no effect (Mk. 7:11-13). Jesus (God in flesh) couldn't do many miracles in His hometown because of their unbelief (Mt. 13:58). If we draw near to God He is quick to draw near to us (Jam. 4:8), but He has given us a free will that we might choose Him or reject Him. God doesn't want puppets or slaves; He desires children with free wills that are impassioned to choose Him in all things. The Father didn't go chasing the prodigal son, but was quick to run to him when he saw him returning (Lk. 15:20). I believe that God can be all-powerful, but He has chosen not to be for the sake of being a loving Father.

Is God omniscient? I believe that He can be, but He has chosen not to be. He says that our sins and our lawless deeds He remembers no more forever (Jer. 31:34; Heb. 8:12; 10:17). He has chosen not to know them. The first man of faith mentioned in the Bible is a man named Abel. Abel gave God the first and the best, but God never commanded him to do so. God 'respected' Abel's offering. The Hebrew word for 'respected' is "HSRN 8159, שָׁעָה shaʿah, shaw-aw´; a primitive root; *to gaze at or about* (properly, for help); by implication, *to inspect, consider, compassionate, be nonplussed* (as looking around in amazement) or *bewildered*." God was surprised with Abel's offering (Gen. 4:4). When Joshua needed more time in the battlefield he requested that God give it to him and God 'heeded the voice of a man' (Josh. 10:14). David's tent was David's idea and God liked it. The tabernacle of Moses was God's command, but David's idea was God's true heart. When it says of God that He knows all of the hairs on our heads, it is a term of endearment and care, not of His sovereignty. Paul told those on the boat that was about to sink to listen to him and trust him and not "a hair on their heads" would be lost. I wonder if anyone lost a literal hair in the shipwreck? God changes His mind, but He never changes His character. If you can appeal to His character of mercy He will quickly change His mind concerning actions. Religious people will never change their minds, but will often change their character in an attempt to remain bound to their words. If God works things out for good in our lives, I think it means He has to 'work some things out'. The fact He has to work things out implies that there are several possibilities that we are in control of, or others are in control of. God is not limited to time or the dimensions of time, as we know it. He is quantum in His abilities. He told Nicodemus that He came from heaven, was going to heaven, and was in heaven right now (Jn. 3:13). Is it God's providential will for a child to be born when a woman is raped by some wicked, self-seeking man? Is it the will of an uncaring, sovereign God. Or is God a loving Father who goes to the place of human conception and chooses to know that child in that place before they were formed in their mother's womb? Is it a sovereign God who determines horrific acts of pain, or a loving Father who turns what was not His will to a testimony of His amazing grace?

Is God omnipresent? Is He present everywhere? Many quote the psalmist when he said he could not go anywhere that God would not be found.

Psalms 139:7-8 Where can I go from Your Spirit? Or where can I flee from Your presence? If I ascend into heaven, You are there; if I make my bed in hell (sheol), behold, You are there.

In these verses the psalmist says He would find God in heaven and he would find God in hell. Hell in this verse is Sheol, the realm of the dead. Does God live in the realm of the dead? If God lived there could it be called the realm of the dead? Does God live everywhere or is He an intimate Father who promises never to leave the psalmist? The psalmist knows that wherever he goes God will be, because God never leaves the psalmist. This is why the grave cannot hold the psalmist.

Romans 8:38-39 For I am persuaded that neither death nor life, nor angels nor principalities nor powers, nor things present nor things to come, nor height nor depth, nor any other created thing, shall be able to separate us from the love of God which is in Christ Jesus our Lord.

I don't believe that it is sovereignty that makes God who He is. There is something that is more powerful than His ability to be sovereign. It is His identity as Father. He gives life, breath, and all things to all people. This is an action of intimacy and endearment, not mere strength. I don't believe that God wants to be God. He is God, but He wants us to know Him as Father. It is through a Father/son, Father/daughter relationship that we can receive His divine guidance for life. It is both specific and providential, but it is intimate and real. He loves His children and delights in their course of life in this earth. Our perception of God influences our ability to hear Him. Sons and daughters of God will hear Him more readily and clearly than mere subjects and slaves.

2. Hindrances in Receiving Divine Guidance

Divine guidance is hearing God and responding to what He says.

I must state it again, it is like dancing with God. Our view of God will greatly affect our ability to dance with Him. If we view Him as impersonal, uncaring, and bound to rigid rules of right and wrong, we will dance a dance of slavery. Our view of God will greatly affect our ability to hear Him and receive His direction in our lives.

Our view of ourselves will also affect our ability to receive divine guidance. If we are self-seeking in our ways we will not be able to receive His direction easily. Selfishness is a hindrance to hearing and responding to God. If we don't want to hear Him, we will not hear Him. If we want to receive God's guidance, we will seek to hear Him. We will be people who love Him and want to have a relationship with Him in all things. In order to receive God's guidance we must listen to what He says. A willingness to obey is a primary condition for guidance.

2 Timothy 3:16-17 All Scripture is given by inspiration of God, and is profitable for doctrine, for reproof, for correction, for instruction in righteousness, that the man of God may be complete, thoroughly equipped for every good work.

Scripture is a testimony of things that God has said in the past. It is filled with statements of truth and truly-stated statements. When these things are put together in their entirety they present a great testimony concerning the truth of God. Scripture is filled with the errors of men and the direction of God that turns all things for good. Scripture is a witness to the voice of God and it is a witness to who God really is. Scripture is not our teacher. The Holy Spirit is our teacher, but Scripture is a witness to the voice of God in our lives. We look to Scripture to learn what God's voice sounds like so we won't be deceived by voices that sound good, but violate the true character, nature, way, power and authority of who God really is.

In order to pass the test of Scripture, anything written must be profitable for our doctrine. That is our way of life. It is not merely profitable for teaching, but for our way of life. Scripture should be a witness to our lifestyles. When our lifestyle is not reflected in the words of Scripture, we are in error somewhere in our lives. This is true for every word from God in our lives. When God speaks He is not merely interested in telling us things to do. He wants us to experience the wonder of being a testimony of His character, nature, way, power, and authority. He wants us to be children who reveal who our Father is to the world around us.

All Scripture is also profitable for reproof. We must understand this through a paradigm of New Covenant, not one of Old Covenant law. The proof of life is within those who believe. Christ in us is the hope of glory (Col. 1:27). I believe that true reproof is to activate the testimony of Christ within us. To use a good American or English idiom, the 'proof is in the pudding', and all things expressed by God are meant to manifest Christ's life and character within us.

All Scripture is profitable for correction. Correction is a means of staying in the path of life. It is not about being right versus being wrong. It is a matter of staying in the path of life and not taking a path that will cause harm. If there is a high mountain road with a sharp curve in the road and people are crashing over the mountainside, it would be foolish to park an ambulance or a funeral hearse at the bottom of the mountain. The road needs some measure of correction to keep the cars in the path of life. Putting up a guardrail could be a measure of correction. The guardrail doesn't mean that the drivers of the cars are bad; it is a means of needed correction in the road to assure that cars remain in the path of life. A greater measure of correction would be to drill a tunnel through the mountain so that cars can drive through the mountain in safety and avoid the dangerous curve at the top of the mountain all together. The tunnel is not an indication that people are bad or that the cars are bad. It is a means of correction that keeps everyone in the path of life. Just as Scripture is meant to aid in bringing God's correction to our lives, any direction of God will bring correction to our lives. His guidance will keep us in the path of life.

All Scripture is profitable for righteousness. This is not the means of being right. It is a testimony of being dependent upon God in all things. It is a testimony of a right relationship with God in all things. God's guidance keeps us rightly joined to Him in everything.

All of these things serve to help us grow and to become complete and thoroughly equipped for every good work in life. God's guidance in our lives is the same. God wants us to be complete and ready for everything we face in life. All of these attributes of guidance are good instruction and they produce good testimonies in our lives, but to receive any aspect of these things means we must want them. We must willingly receive God's direction to our way of life, His admonitions to bring Christ out of us, His correction to keep us in the path of life, and His influence that causes us to depend upon Him in all things. If we are self-seeking we will refuse these things. If we want to receive His guidance we must be willing to obey what He says. A willingness to obey is a primary condition for God's guidance.

If we are willing to do God's will, we'll know. When we are hesitant to ask God for His direction it is an indication that we don't really want His guidance. If we are defensive to our way we are resisting His way in our lives. If we fight with Him we are not seeking to hear Him in a way that will give us His divine guidance. We are hindering His divine guidance through our own selfish attitudes and actions.

God's direction in our lives will often invoke a willingness to yield on our part. That willingness is inspired by faith that only works through a revelation of love. Loving God is testified by seeking Him, but when we love things more than Him those things can sway our hearts to look in the wrong direction concerning His love. It is a matter of self-focus and self-seeking. Selfishness will only empower our hearts and minds to resist His direction in our lives. When we resist what God is saying to us we begin to justify why we resist Him. We become defensive towards His instruction and often substitute His direction for ideas of our own. We try to convince ourselves that our ideas are something that God has placed within our hearts, or He has given to us in some way. When we insist on our own way, God's cure may be an overabundant supply of what we are asking for, until we wish we never had it.

Numbers 11:18-20 "Then you shall say to the people, 'Sanctify yourselves for tomorrow, and you shall eat meat; for you have wept in the hearing of the LORD, saying, "Who will give us meat to eat? For it was well with us in Egypt." Therefore the LORD will give you meat, and you shall eat. You shall eat, not one day, nor two days, nor five days, nor ten days, nor twenty days, but for a whole month, until it comes out of your nostrils and becomes loathsome to you, because you have despised the LORD who is among you, and have wept before Him, saying, "Why did we ever come up out of Egypt?"'

In this story, the children of Israel were complaining in their hearts towards the present situation of only eating manna in the wilderness. Their hearts desired the things of the past and God was allowing them to have their own way in the matter.

Numbers 11:32-34 And the people stayed up all that day, all that night, and all the next day, and gathered the quail (he who gathered least gathered ten homers); and they spread them out for themselves all around the camp. But while the meat was still between their teeth, before it was chewed, the wrath of the LORD was aroused against the people, and the LORD struck the people with a very great plague. So he called the name of that place Kibroth Hattaavah, because there they buried the people who had yielded to craving.

God caused the wind to blow and the quail to be within the reach of the children of Israel. Just because God allows something to be accessible doesn't mean He wants us to take hold of it. When the children took the meat it was death to them. They had insisted on their own way and God had allowed their own way to be an easy possibility. God wasn't trying to trick them. He was revealing their hearts to them.

James 1:12-15 Blessed is the man who endures temptation; for when he has been proved, he will receive the crown of life which the Lord has promised to those who love Him. Let no one say when he is tempted, "I am tempted by God"; for God cannot be tempted by evil, nor does He Himself tempt anyone. But each one is tempted when he is drawn away by his own desires and enticed. Then, when desire has conceived, it gives birth to sin; and sin, when it is fullgrown, brings forth death.

Is there anything in us that is willing to compromise in our character to receive what we want? When we put the end as more important than the means, we are willing to compromise in the means by which we attain the end. God's promises are not more important than God's character. Being children of God that exhibit His character, nature, way, power, and authority is a testimony to the likeness and the image of God in the earth. God's promises, or our perceptions of His promises, are not more important than Him.

If we insist on our own way we are going to get it! As I have presented, God is not trying to trick us. He wants us to know what is in our own hearts. Selfishness is a hindrance to receiving God's guidance in our lives. Hearing God includes the aspect of responding to Him. If we are practicing not responding, we are practicing not hearing Him.

If we are disobedient to God in an area of our lives we can hardly expect Him to direct us. We all wrestle with obedience at times, but willful disobedience will for sure hinder our ability to see God work things out for His will in our lives. God expects us to seek Him and to draw near to Him. He is quick to respond to those who seek Him, but He will not chase us in our running. The father of the prodigal son waited for him daily, but he didn't chase after him while he was running from the father's will. God will go looking for a lost sheep, but a lost sheep isn't someone who is defensive and aggressively running from God. They are someone who doesn't know where they are. God comes to us in our hesitation, but He won't come to us while we are being self-defensive and running from Him. He will call to us, but He will wait for us to turn in His direction, for He will never force Himself upon us. However, an instant of hesitation and turning in His direction invokes a quick response of His love in our direction.

James 4:8-10 Draw near to God and He will draw near to you. Cleanse your hands, you sinners; and purify your hearts, you

43

double-minded. Lament and mourn and weep! Let your laughter be turned to mourning and your joy to gloom. Humble yourselves in the sight of the Lord, and He will lift you up.

God looks for the hungry. He looks for the humble. He is quick to draw near to those who draw near to Him. As we submit to guidance, we find Him taking initiative in our lives. He will work things out for those who sincerely turn toward Him. He will adjust and rearrange things in our lives where we have been off track in some way if we honestly look to seek for His help.

Insincerity is another pitfall in the process of hearing God. We demonstrate insincerity when we want God's approval to do what we have already determined in our hearts to do. We shut ourselves off from genuine guidance by following our own desires and coating them with a veneer of pretended obedience. I can't tell you how many times I have seen the issue of insincerity present in those who pretend to want His direction in their lives. If we come to God with a strong will in our hearts it is hard for us to yield to His will. If we say we are looking for God's direction in our lives, but we have gone to twenty different counselors and have not responded to a word that any have given us, we aren't looking for guidance. We might just be looking for someone to agree with what we have already decided in our hearts to do.

Isaiah 29:13 Therefore the LORD said: "Inasmuch as these people draw near to Me with their mouths and honor Me with their lips, but have removed their hearts far from Me, and their fear toward Me is taught by the commandment of men,"

Matthew 15:1-9 Then the scribes and Pharisees who were from Jerusalem came to Jesus, saying, "Why do Your disciples transgress the tradition of the elders? For they do not wash their hands when they eat bread." But He answered and said to them, "Why do you also transgress the commandment of God because of your tradition? For God commanded, saying, 'Honor your father and your mother'; and, 'He who curses father or mother, let him be put to death.' But you say, 'Whoever says to his father or mother, "Whatever profit you might have received from me is a gift to God"— then he need not honor his father or mother.' Thus you have made the commandment of God of no effect by your tradition. Hypocrites! Well did Isaiah prophesy about you, saying: 'These people draw near to Me with their mouth, and honor Me with their lips, but their heart is far from Me. 'And in vain they worship Me, teaching as doctrines the commandments of men.'"

One can obey without really submitting, but someone who is submissive will always obey. Submission is an attitude of the heart, while obedience can be merely an imitation of submission and is a testimony of insincerity. The Pharisees performed religious acts, pretending to seek God, but only performed those acts for their own benefit. They prided themselves in being 'spiritual', but they didn't want to do what God said.

Sometimes human desires are masked as guidance in order to make rebellion palatable to others and us. The result is self-deception and a rejection of true guidance. If we are seeking counsel and we say God said something, we have already decided that God has said something so how can anything else be injected? We might know what God said, but we might not have any idea what it really means. Revelation is one thing; interpretation and application of that revelation are other aspects of understanding what God said. If we are adamant that what we heard means a certain thing already, we are not open to hearing anything beyond what we have determined to be God's voice. This can likely be an aspect of insincerity before God.

Matthew 7:21-23 "Not everyone who says to Me, 'Lord, Lord,' shall enter the kingdom of heaven, but he who does the will of My Father in heaven. Many will say to Me in that day, 'Lord, Lord, have we not prophesied in Your name, cast out demons in Your name, and done many wonders in Your name?' And then I will declare to them, 'I never knew you; depart from Me, you who practice lawlessness!'"

In these verses there is a hidden Hebrew idiom. The phrase 'Lord, Lord' is unique to the Hebrew language, though it was written in the Greek language, the gospel of Matthew was a book written to the Jews. The first mention of this phrase is found when God revealed His glory to Moses on Mt. Sinai (Ex. 34:6). In the Stone's edition of the English translation of the Torah, the rabbinical commentaries state that this double mention of the 'Lord' is part of Jewish idiom speech. They write that the first 'Lord' means that God is the one who forgives us of our sins before we do them, knowing the full extent of everything we will do. The second 'Lord' implies that He is the one who forgives us after we sin knowing the full extent of everything we have ever done. This 'Lord, Lord' phrase then refers to a strong relationship with God based upon His love. Those in this Matthew 7 text did the works of God, but had no revelation of the love of God. They didn't know that it was about a relationship with God. They thought it was about doing the works of God. When we exhibit this kind of insincerity, we pride ourselves in being spiritual, but we don't want to do what God says. We want to be known for the things we do for God, but we don't want to really know God.

Isaiah 4:1 And in that day seven women shall take hold of one man, saying, "We will eat our own food and wear our own apparel; only let us be called by your name, to take away our reproach."

In this verse of Isaiah there are those who want to receive the benefits of the name of God, but they don't want to change. They don't want to eat His food or wear His clothes. They are more concerned with their own personal desires and their self-seeking, self-motivated testimonies. I believe that the prophet Isaiah was talking about the full seven-fold dispensations that led to the day of Jesus. The true fulfillment of the desires of the nations – depicted in Adam, Noah and the patriarchs, Moses and the testimony, David and the monarchy, the kingdom's fall to apathy and captivity, the restoration of Ezra and Nehemiah, and the Pharisaic system – were all meant to be transformed by life in Christ. In the day of Jesus, some say they don't want to change. They just want the benefits of His name. This is insincerity.

Psalms 81:13-16 "Oh, that My people would listen to Me, That Israel would walk in My ways! I would soon subdue their enemies, And turn My hand against their adversaries. The haters of the LORD would pretend submission to Him, But their fate would endure forever. He would have fed them also with the finest of wheat; And with honey from the rock I would have satisfied you."

Pretend submission is mere superficial obedience and it is the testimony of an insincere heart. This is a hindrance to the true guidance of God in our lives. We must allow God to cut away the insincere motives of our hearts so we can find the true voice of God in our lives. If we can eliminate our hindrances of disobedience and insincerity we can hear God for the direction of our lives. The voice of God doesn't inspire or condone self-seeking, disobedience, or insincerity. God wants to free us all from our self-seeking, disobedience, and insincerity to the liberty of His will.

Impatience can be a huge hinderance to the process of God's guidance in our lives. Patience is a partner to faith in our journey of receiving God's words and responding to His will and way. Faith comes by hearing God speak to us, but patience enables us to continue to hear God throughout the process. Faith doesn't come by the logos of God. It comes by the rhema. It doesn't come by standing fast on the things that God has said to us in the past (logos). It is a supernatural result of hearing God in the moment (rhema). We must stay in the place of continuing to hear God speak to us in order to continue in the place of faith. Because of this, we can see how important patience can be as a partner to faith. It is through faith and patience that we inherit the promises of God in our lives.

Hebrews 6:11-12 And we desire that each one of you show the same diligence to the full assurance of hope until the end, that you do not become sluggish, but imitate those who through faith and patience inherit the promises.

In the parable of the seed cast upon the good soil, it was the fruit of hearing God in conjunction with patience that caused the word to take root and grow. Patience is a key partner to faith in the process of God's guidance in our life.

Luke 8:15 "But the ones that fell on the good ground are those who, having heard the word with a noble and good heart, keep it and bear fruit with patience."

In the process of guidance, patience is the testimony of faith and it is the very proving ground of faith. It is faith and patience working together in our lives that produces the perfect completed work of God in our lives.

James 1:3-4 ...knowing that the testing of your faith produces patience. But let patience have its perfect work, that you may be perfect and complete, lacking nothing.

Patience is part of the process of God's guidance in our lives. If we choose shortcuts in our journey we will come short of the destination of our journey. Patience is a key ingredient in our ability to hear God, to continue to hear God, to hear God again, and to continually respond to Him. Another word for patience is the word longsuffering. It is part of the fruit of the Spirit in our lives (Gal. 5:22). Stirring up the Holy Spirit within our hearts and clinging to Him in all things will activate the process of patience in our lives. God doesn't want us to escape our circumstances in life. He wants for us to find the process of His divine guidance in the midst of every circumstance of our journey. Patience is a key ingredient to hearing and walking in response to God and impatience is a big hindrance to His guidance in our lives.

Another hindrance to God's guidance in our lives is self-sufficiency. It is perhaps the most dangerous hindrance of all. It can come disguised under the pretense of obedience to God or knowing God's word. The Pharisees and Sadducees of Jesus's day were bound to the hindrance of self-sufficiency. They prided themselves in their ability to be right and to know what was right. Their righteousness was self-righteousness and it was a testimony of their own self-sufficiency. Their responses to Jesus were ones of constantly defending their own preconceived understandings of God. The Pharisees couldn't see who Jesus was because they were dependent upon their past understanding of God more than their present experience with Him. This was a hindrance of self-sufficiency in their lives.

The key characteristic of a surrendered will is a determination to set aside its own will for the will of God. Jesus demonstrated His dependence upon His heavenly Father when He was about to be crucified. As He prayed in the garden His will was yielded to His heavenly Father and His sufficiency was dependent upon Him.

Luke 22:42 ... "Father, if it is Your will, take this cup away from Me; nevertheless not My will, but Yours, be done."

Pride is a real, but subtle, hindrance to guidance. There are many forms of pride. There is an obvious arrogant and stubborn pride. There is also a pride called false humility. I have seen many Christians fall into the trap of both of these forms of pride. Some pride themselves in their ability to hear God. They become very bold with the things that God has said, or they perceive that He has said, and they are not willing to yield in their interpretation or their application of what they believe to have heard from God. I believe that we very often hear 100% of the revelation God speaks to us, but on a good day our understanding of what the words mean or how they apply are likely only 1% to 5% of what was really said. On an exceptional day we may understand 10% of His words to our hearts.

Sometimes pride causes us to have an attitude of needing to be naturally convinced before we embrace God's thoughts to be true. Many people say that if God will show them clearly, then they will believe. This is not the way of faith. While we may say, "Show me and I'll believe"; God says, "Believe and you will see!" The people of Berea were these kind of people.

Acts 17:11 These were more fair-minded than those in Thessalonica,

*in that they received the word with all readiness, and searched the
Scriptures daily to find out whether these things were so.*

These people in Berea believed in their hearts and then they searched
the Scriptures to see that what they were hearing was true. They were able
to see truth in the Scriptures because they first believed in their hearts.
They didn't search the Scriptures to see what they should believe. They
believed God and then they searched Scripture to understand what they
were receiving faith to believe. They were eager and willing to receive
the things of God and were not bound by pride in their hearing.

Another type of pride is that of false humility. It is often a very
religious form of pride. When we do something good and people
compliment us on our actions or our service in some way, do we reject
the compliment and say, "It's not me! It's all Jesus! He is the one who
gets the glory. I'm not anything, it is all Him." When I hear that I want
to say, "It wasn't that good!" You see, sometimes we pull the false
humility card and false humility is really another form of pride. It is
Jesus, but it is also us and Jesus. It is Christ in us that is the hope of
glory and false humility will manifest a form of pride that will hinder
God's guidance in our lives.

Impatience, self-sufficiency, and pride are all hindrances to God's
voice and guidance in our lives. We must allow the Holy Spirit to empower
us to be patient, God-dependent, and God-yielding in all things.

3. Guidance From God Is Subject To God

We have been given some great and marvelous treasures. The first
and foremost is a precious relationship with God whereby His Holy Spirit
lives within us. We hear His voice, but we don't always discern His voice
correctly. God knows our challenge and He has made provisions to help
us discern what He is saying in our lives. He has given us another gift
that is great and precious as well. We have the gift of God's written word.
When we learn to understand God's word in the light of His person, His
written world will help guide our emotions, feelings, impressions and

any other signs or leadings that we receive in life. We must understand that God's written word has not been given to us so that we will merely know what to do or how to act. God's written word has been given to us as a witness to the voice of God and we must study it in the light of knowing who God is as a person. It is a testimony of real people in real relationships and with real encounters with God. It is a testimony of man's successes and failures, and God's faithfulness and love in all things. When we hear God, God's voice is subject to the testimony of what He has been like in the past. He is the same yesterday, today, and forever and the testimonies of Him in the past are a solid witness to who He is today. God will not deviate from His character, nature, way, power, or authority, and His written word is a testimony to who He is.

When we hear God we hear Him clearly, but we very often interpret what He has said in a wrong way. We must submit any revelation given to us by God to the witness of His written word. God's spoken word is measured by His written word. This does not mean that His spoken word is measured by our misinterpretation of Scripture. The written word of God is not our teacher; it is a witness to our teacher. Our teacher is the Holy Spirit and the written word helps us understand His voice more clearly. The written word doesn't measure who God is; who God is measures the written word. However, the written word is a testimony used by the Holy Spirit in teaching us who God is.

John 5:32 There is another who bears witness of Me, and I know that the witness which He witnesses of Me is true.

John 5:39 You search the Scriptures, for in them you think you have eternal life; and these are they which testify of Me.

1 John 2:27 But the anointing which you have received from Him abides in you, and you do not need that anyone teach you; but as the same anointing teaches you concerning all things, and is true, and is not a lie, and just as it has taught you, you will abide in Him.

My wife and I have been married for over 38 years. We have grown

51

in our relationship with one another. My wife's spoken word is measured by her written word. Who I have discovered her to be is a testimony to who she is today. If you were to tell me that she said something she didn't really say, I would be able to recognize the discrepancy in what you say. I know who she is and therefore I know what she might say. This is true in our relationship with God. We must stand fast upon the expressed word rather than what we perceive to be an expression of Him. This means we must study His written word in order to know who He is. The Holy Spirit Himself yields to the written word. He never acts outside of, or in contradiction to, the Word of God.

Psalms 138:2 I will worship toward Your holy temple, and praise Your name for Your lovingkindness and Your truth; for You have magnified Your word above all Your name.

God's word is not the legalistic character of His expressions, but the substance of who He is in His expressions. God will change His mind, because He can never change His character. If we give Him a reason for mercy, He will be merciful and relent from words He has spoken. His word is a written testimony to His character, not our dogmatic interpretations of words He has spoken. Religious people take the words that God has said in Scripture and use them for their own religious gain. They take their own interpretations of God's word and they are willing to change their character to defend their own understanding of those words. They refuse to change their words and they are willing to bend or change their character to defend their views of God's written word. We must study God's written word to know the character of who He is and to stay true to the character of His voice in discerning what He is saying to us in our lives.

The word of God will never lie, but a verse lifted out of context can lead us astray. When we are unstable or untaught we can twist what God has said to our own destruction. The religious of Jesus's day twisted His words, as was foretold by the Psalmist.

Psalms 56:4-5 In God (I will praise His word), in God I have put my trust; I will not fear. What can flesh do to me? All day they twist my words; all their thoughts are against me for evil.

The unstable and untaught in the church of the first century twisted the words of Paul to their own destruction.

2 Peter 3:14-16 Therefore, beloved, looking forward to these things, be diligent to be found by Him in peace, without spot and blameless; and consider that the longsuffering of our Lord is salvation – as also our beloved brother Paul, according to the wisdom given to him, has written to you, as also in all his epistles, speaking in them of these things, in which are some things hard to understand, which those who are untaught and unstable twist to their own destruction, as they do also the rest of the Scriptures.

It is possible to read the Word of God out of context and therefore be misled. Jesus said that unless we hate our fathers and our mothers we cannot be His disciples, but in the context of the entire word we find that He expects us to honor our fathers and our mothers in all things. He was not advocating that anyone hate their father or their mother, but that our love and honor for God would excel what we know to be the expected place of love and honor in all things.

We must study God's word in order to know who God is. We cannot be lazy in our approach towards God's word and expect to properly understand His voice in our hearts. No team of doctors undertakes open-heart surgery without being thoroughly acquainted with every available knowledge and skill in that area. We must study every expression of God we know. Something that has been expressed of God is the logos of God (Greek for 'word that has been expressed'). Scripture is logos; human examples in the faith, such as God-given authority in our lives, are also logos of God. What God has formed in us in a former time is a logos of God. Anything that has been expressed of God is a witness to what is being expressed by God in our lives. Faith comes by the NOW expression of God in our lives, but interpretation of what is being expressed is aided by what has been expressed in the past.

4. How Does Guidance Occur?

God wants to communicate with you and He wants to give guidance in your life. Think about this, someone who loves you very much wants to help you. God, the one who loves you more than anyone, wants to help you find direction in life. That direction is not so you will have a life that is very busy doing good things or a life consumed with ministry activities or so-called 'Christian' activities. God wants you to know Him. He wants you to know who you are in relation to Him. He wants you to realize who other people are. God wants to give you guidance for the sake of being part of the family of God, knowing the members of the family of God, and finally fulfilling the purpose of the family name in the world.

God's guidance in your life is like dancing. God wants to dance with you and He is the leading partner in the relationship. In giving you guidance, God will often order your steps so you will be in the right place at the right time. This is often called providential guidance. A good example of His providential guidance is found in the book of Psalms.

> *Psalms 37:3-5 Trust in the LORD, and do good;*
> *Dwell in the land, and feed on His faithfulness.*
> *Delight yourself also in the LORD,*
> *And He shall give you the desires of your heart.*
> *Commit your way to the LORD,*
> *Trust also in Him,*
> *And He shall bring it to pass.*

We can trust that God will guide our lives when we trust in the Lord, seek to do good, make it our aim to be responsible in life before Him, know that we live on His faithful love in our lives, and we delight ourselves in the Him in all things. He will literally put desires in our hearts. Human beings are not so good at doing what they are told. They don't make good slaves, cattle, or horses. They make fantastic children of God when their hearts are filled with the desires of God.

I don't know about you, but I am not always good at doing what I am told. I have learned the skill of doing what I am told, but I had to first embrace a desire to be willing to do what I am told. It is the desire of the heart that impassions us to do the things we do in life. Since I am not good at doing what I am told, I have asked God not to merely tell me what to do. I have asked Him to tell me 'want' to do. I have asked Him not to be Lord of the 'what to' of my life, but to be Lord of the 'want to' of my life. I have given Him permission to go deep and be the Lord of my heart. This is the open door to the providential guidance of God in our lives. When we trust Him, take responsibility before Him, know we depend upon His love, and we delight ourselves in Him, we can increasingly trust the desires of our hearts. In this God promises safety.

Psalms 37:23-24 The steps of a good man are ordered by the LORD,
*   And He delights in his way.*
*   Though he fall, he shall not be utterly cast down;*
*   For the LORD upholds him with His hand.*

When we walk in the way I have described, we can be assured that the Lord delights in our course of life. Even if we make a mistake and fall, God will be there to pick us up. He takes what was intended for evil in our lives and works it out for good.

Romans 8:26-28 Likewise the Spirit also helps in our weaknesses. For we do not know what we should pray for as we ought, but the Spirit Himself makes intercession for us with groanings which cannot be uttered. Now He who searches the hearts knows what the mind of the Spirit is, because He makes intercession for the saints according to the will of God. And we know that all things work together for good to those who love God, to those who are the called according to His purpose.

In addition to God's providential guidance in our lives, God also wants to speak with us specifically and in very special ways. This could be called special guidance or specific guidance in our lives. This can include things like personal prophecy. When God speaks specifically, the highest form of communication is spoken within the human heart. Even when we receive a personal prophecy from someone, the word only becomes specific when the person receiving the word hears the voice of God within his or her own heart. God may speak to us through an out loud audible voice. When I survey a spiritually-minded group of people, I find that about 20% of the group will have heard God's audible voice at some time in their life. This is not a more spiritual way to hear God. It is just one of many ways that God speaks to us in specific and special ways. Even when we hear an audible voice it must witness with the voice of God in our hearts. God wants to talk to us through internal impressions, visions, dreams, angelic encounters, prophecy, supernatural interventions, and many other specific ways.

When God speaks to us we must be willing to dance the dance of His guidance in our lives. We hear Him specifically and we trust Him providentially. We trust Him providentially and we hear Him specifically. In all of this it is a matter of relationship with Him and it must bear the life-giving fruit of knowing Him in our lives.

God wants to walk with us with an intimate relationship. Guidance is like dancing. God is the one who leads and we respond to His voice, His direction, and His movements in our lives. Most guidance from God happens without us even being aware of it. God loves us and He wants to guide our lives, not so we will know what to do but so we will know Him in all things. Hearing God and responding to Him should be a natural part of our lives. Our heavenly Father loves us and He wants to guide our lives. Shouldn't this be a natural thing? It should be a part of a normal life as a human being. When we commit our lives to Him, He directs our steps. How do we commit our lives to Him? When we say in our hearts that we are going to be a man or a woman of God, God is faithful to direct us. We may make some mistakes, but if our hearts are right towards Him He will work things out for us. God doesn't want us to be some kind of puppet. He doesn't want us to be a slave. When we have a relationship with God we must know that He also trusts us and He wants for us to walk in a relationship with Him.

Jesus charged His disciples to have faith. When they did not have faith He rebuked them for having little faith. Faith comes by hearing God in our hearts. When we hear God faith happens. I don't believe that there is really such a thing as big faith or little faith. Faith as small as a mustard seed is sufficient for great things. The issue is our confidence in faith. It is our confidence in what we have heard God say. It is our confidence in what God is saying. Confidence in faith is manifested in our willingness to put our full assurance in even the smallest measure of His voice. The truth is that even if we make a mistake God will work it out for us. He knows we are trying and He knows that we want to be obedient to His voice. We cannot embrace the hindrances I have addressed earlier and simply expect God to work everything out, however. Sometimes our disobedience, pride, insincerity, self-seeking, impatience or some other personal agenda can cause us to suffer the consequence of our errors, but God still wants to give us direction in our lives. Some guidance from God comes easy and in a straight path in our lives, while other guidance comes in a roundabout way. Our path with God is like the globe – a sphere. We can get anywhere from anywhere, but some paths take a longer time. It is like a ship on an ocean, when our lives are off course we don't go back to the port, we simply turn the wheel and adjust our course. A journey that includes errors in our course can be adjusted and we can be directed back to destiny.

In discovering God's guidance in our lives, we must make a commitment to God's world. We must recognize that His world is our world and that our world is His. We must separate our lives unto Him. This is not a life of abstinence from the things of the flesh; it is a life of indulgence in His Spirit. We must be filled with His Spirit, embrace the passion of His Spirit, seek to do the works of the Spirit, and live lives that are filled with the character and way of His Spirit. We were not merely saved from hell, but salvaged into a passionate relationship with God. Holiness is a separation unto God, not merely a separation from the things of the world. When we embrace the fullness of God in His Spirit we put to death the deeds of the flesh. This is the secret to our commitment to God's way.

We must trust God in His word and His promises. We must trust what He says in our lives and what He has said in the past. Abraham didn't just believe what God said; He trusted God said it and He trusted God. Many people trust God's prophecies and promises more than they trust the fact that God spoke them. Faith comes by hearing God speak personally in our hearts. Faith comes by naturally trusting the supernatural breath of God.

To receive God's guidance we must embrace a lifestyle of prayer. This is not just having times of doing the work of prayer; it is a personal recognition of a seven-day per week, twenty-four hour per day, relationship with God. We cannot just have a 'Facebook' relationship with God. We must embrace a face-to-face relationship with Him. We must stir up our spirits with the life of the Holy Spirit within us. We must position our souls to be subject to our spirits. We don't want to embrace a rigid, disciplined life of prayer. We need a fluid relationship with Him. We must walk in an intimate fellowship with God in life. God is our friend, our Father, our covenant Partner, and our Brother. He is compassionate towards us and passionate about us. He wants to communicate with us. When we commit our way to Him, trust Him, and embrace a face-to-face relationship with Him in life we can expect His divine guidance to be very evident in who we are and what we do.

Hearing God is an issue of intimacy. True intimacy with someone isn't merely dependent upon their affection for you. True intimacy is connected to your covenant towards the other person. If you put conditions upon the relationship, there will be conditions upon your hearing the other person. In this, your personal character plays a big role. Your personal integrity will set a foundation for rightly interpreting God's direction in your life. This means you must make it your aim to know the heart of the One you are seeking to hear. God is very good. He has revealed Himself in the past and we have a witness to His voice in our present. That witness is the word of His Scripture. Scripture was not given so we will know what to do or how to act. It was given so we have a good witness to recognizing and understanding the voice of God in our own lives. It reveals the character, nature, way, power, and authority of who God is. If we don't seek to know God in His written word we will fail in knowing Him correctly through His spoken word in our lives. It is like tuning into a radio station. If we don't know the sound of the correct frequency we are apt to tune into a wrong channel and think it is the voice of God. God will even allow us to hear things that will test the integrity of our own hearts in regard to our relationship with Him.

The present generation is faced with a big challenge. We live in a day of expedient information and it is difficult sometimes to know what to believe. I have discovered much of the present generation doesn't believe that the Bible is necessary in discerning God's voice. They complain that it is difficult to understand, but the true case is they are often too lazy to learn God's language. They expect God to speak their language, but God expects them to learn His. If we move to a foreign country we must expect to have to learn the culture, the way, and the language of the country, since we have now become residents. We cannot remain in our old country's mindset and expect to understand the culture and system we have moved to. The same is true for us in the kingdom of God. We are now residents of heaven and we must learn the culture, way, and language of God. I am not talking about legally standing on the words of Scripture as we think they are stated. I am talking about learning the heart and language of God, in the words He has inspired in the Scriptures. They were written for the sake of our way of life, bringing Christ out of us, keeping us in the path of life, and empowering us to be dependent upon a personal relationship with Him. His word has been given so we will hear Him correctly and become complete as His children and thoroughly equipped for every good work (2 Tim. 3:16-17).

When it comes to guidance from God, we often fall short in receiving His direction because we seek the wrong thing from Him. Very often our desire is to get out of some circumstance or be relieved of some symptom in our lives. We think we seek God, but we are really seeking to get out of our present situations. Our circumstances, or symptoms, in life don't need to be healed. It is most often a root in our lives that caused the symptom that is the real issue. For this reason we must study to know who God is and what He is like so we don't find ourselves making illegitimate requests with illegitimate expectations. If we simply hear Him and don't respond to what He says we cannot blame Him when our house falls down. The man or woman who builds their house upon the rock is the man or woman who doesn't merely hear God, but responds to what He says when He says it.

Matthew 7:24-27 "Therefore whoever hears these sayings of Mine, and does them, I will liken him to a wise man who built his house on the rock: and the rain descended, the floods came, and the winds blew and beat on that house; and it did not fall, for it was founded on the rock. But everyone who hears these sayings of Mine, and does not do them, will be like a foolish man who built his house on the sand: and the rain descended, the floods came, and the winds blew and beat on that house; and it fell. And great was its fall."

We must learn to hear God's voice correctly and we must learn to respond to His voice in our lives. This is essential to receiving His guidance. The Bible has been given to us to assist us in hearing God's voice correctly. Many people in the present generation question the Bible, thus they are vulnerable to deception. Many people use the Bible as a tool of legalism and twist its inspiration by the religious interpretations of men; this too makes them vulnerable to deception. Let me give some basic statements concerning the Scriptures that may help you in embracing its purpose and validity in your course of hearing God in your life.

How Can We Trust The Bible?

1. The Scriptures were inspired by God, or literally God-breathed (2 Tim. 3:16), thus the Bible is not a single book, but a book of books written by 40 or more authors in three different languages, over a period of 1500 years, and it reveals the person God in a consistent, constant, and confirming way.

2. The voice of the Holy Spirit within you is the greatest witness to the Bible's authority and life – God speaks to your spirit not your soul. Looking into the written word inspires the life-giving word of

God's Spirit into your spirit. A prosperous spirit floods the soul to give understanding. It is witnessed by life and interpreted through the Tree of Life and not the tree of the knowledge of good and evil.

3. Holy Spirit is your Teacher – Not Scripture (Jn. 5:39). The Scripture is a witness to the Voice of the Holy Spirit, but without the Scriptures you are susceptible to false voices and false teaching.

4. The Scripture is filled with truly stated statements and statements of truth to reveal a big picture of truth. Verses by themselves can be truly stated statements of men, but not statements of truth. Other verses are statements of truth by God, but when they are put together in their entirety the truly stated statements and the statements of truth reveal the truth of man's failure and the goodness of who God is.

5. Untaught and unstable people twist the Scripture to their own destruction (2 Pet. 3:16), but that doesn't make Scripture inaccurate, irrelevant, or unnecessary. It means being stable (not offended in relationship with God and men) and taught (wise to the full language of Scripture) will empower you to understand God's word.

6. Truth is understood from different angles, but the purpose of truth is to witness the Voice – Holy Spirit in your life.

7. Without a book testifying of the Author – You are susceptible to any author.

8. The purpose of the Bible is to reveal the Person God, not mere facts about Him.

9. Variations in translations are minor in the big picture of Scripture and all is subject to the voice of the Holy Spirit within you.

10. The Scripture is the written testimony that gives a compass and a bearing to the things that are being heard, written, and kept by the power of the Holy Spirit in your life.

11. Early church writers claimed the Scripture to be the Word of God.

12. People were willing to die for it and did die for it – it must be important and valuable!

13. God intervened to give a dream to a world emperor to preserve the written word before it was lost (Constantine and *the Edict of Toleration*).

14. It is the glory of God to hide secrets and the glory of kings to search them out (Pr. 25:2). God hides things and lazy people never really discover the truth. The Bible is the safe ground in which God has hidden His secrets – His voice to our hearts is the secret to true discovery, but the Bible reveals the ground to look in.

15. Your view of God will determine your interpretation of the Bible. People who misrepresent the Scripture do so because they have a wrong view of God. If one thinks God is angry, mean, lording, legalistic, etc., one's interpretation of Scripture will be filtered through those paradigms. The Bible is not the problem, the interpreter is.

2 Timothy 2:15 Be diligent to present yourself approved to God, a worker who does not need to be ashamed, rightly dividing the word of truth.

5. Your Personal Integrity and Guidance From God

When it comes to hearing the voice of God and His guidance in our lives there is a powerful witness within us. That witness is one of the kingdom of heaven. Jesus said that the kingdom of God isn't about what we see happening around us, but it is a matter of what is happening in us.

Luke 17:20-21 Now when He was asked by the Pharisees when the kingdom of God would come, He answered them and said, "The kingdom of God does not come with observation; nor will they say, 'See here!' or 'See there!' For indeed, the kingdom of God is within you."

The kingdom of God within us is a clear witness to discerning the voice of God in our lives. The apostle Paul said that the kingdom of God is not about what we eat or don't eat, it is not about the things we do or don't do; the kingdom of God is righteousness, peace, and joy in the Holy Spirit (Rom. 14:17). When we hear God, understand what He is saying to us, and begin to apply His words in lives it will be witnessed by righteousness, peace, and joy in the Holy Spirit within our hearts. If these things are not present then we have not heard God's voice.

So what does righteousness in the Holy Spirit look like? I believe that true righteousness is found in believing God. It is a place that is free from condemnation before Him (Rom. 8:1). It is not about doing right things to be justified, but rather knowing that we are justified inspiring us to do right things. It is through a right relationship with God in our hearts that we know true righteousness. Any word or thought that comes to us to condemn us is not a word from God. God's words free us and draw us close to Him in our hearts. A word or thought that pushes us away from God or inspires us to hide from Him in some way is not a word confirmed by the righteousness of the Holy Spirit within our hearts. God will never put upon us something that Jesus has already taken off of us at the cross. Thoughts or words that invoke a rigid legalistic view of having to be right are not a word from God. God is merciful and gracious. He will change His mind, but He will never change His character. His character of mercy will require Him to change His mind as revealed in many testimonies in the Scripture. Someone with a pharisaic or religious mind may demand to be right and will be willing to change their own character for the sake of refusing to change their mind. Any thought or word that supports such a character is not a word from God. A God thought or word will keep us in a right relationship with God and with people. Any word that presses us to hide from God or people in our lives is a word that is not witnessed by righteousness in our hearts. True righteousness is a dependency upon God and others and it causes us to say, "Here I am." It is a confession of "God you are my God!" If a word inspires something else to be god, such as a love for ministry, a material thing, a position of importance, a miracle, deliverance, a change of circumstance, etc. it is at the least a distortion to the voice of God in our lives.

What is peace in the Holy Spirit? Peace is not the absence of conflict; it is having your house in the right place so it remains strong on good days and on bad ones. Peace is where there is no gap between God and us. If we experience a hesitation, a sense of disconnection, or a check of some kind in our heart, this is a caution to a lack of peace. Peace in the Holy Spirit is a witness of the kingdom of God within us.

What about joy? It is in the presence of God that we know the fullness of joy (Ps. 16:11). A thought or a word that robs us of God's joy in our hearts is not a word from God. God is in our world and we are in His. Our hearts witness to His manifest presence in our lives. Any word from God will be witnessed by joy in the Holy Spirit within our hearts.

We can be assured of any word from God by the righteousness, peace, and joy of the Holy Spirit within our hearts. This is a witness of the kingdom of God within us. We must respond to the Holy Spirit within our hearts and seek to live lives that are inspired to depend upon God, be a testimony of Him, and live together with Him in all things.

Another key in receiving guidance from God is to ask legitimate questions. If we already know what God desires, yet we ask for permission to do something that is contrary to His character, nature, way, power, or authority, we will open our hearts to some form of deception.

Proverbs 11:3 The integrity of the upright will guide them, but the perversity of the unfaithful will destroy them.

When we pray for something God has already forbidden in His word, we are likely to get our guidance from the wrong source. This is another reason why it is so important to study God's word to know the character, nature, way, power, and authority of who He is. We must learn the culture of His kingdom and not seek for answers to questions that are outside of the boundaries of His kingdom. We cannot expect His kingdom to come and His will to be done if we are looking for answers in the wrong kingdom and desiring a will that contradicts God's desires.

God is not just the one who gives guidance to our lives; He is the one who wants to give us guidance in life. His guidance is not a shallow thing, but a rich treasure. That rich treasure is a treasure of knowing God. God doesn't just want to give us instructions that help us know what to do. He wants us to know who He is and who we are. We have been given the witness of God's written word so we can know His voice in our lives. Knowing God's written word is a key to discerning His spoken word in our lives. If we don't know what God's voice sounds like we will be susceptible to believe other voices when we hear them. As I have stated many times, the Scripture is not our teacher, the Holy Spirit is; but the Scripture is a clear witness to the voice of the Holy Spirit. The Scriptures testify of Jesus (Jn. 5:39). We must seek to know the Scriptures so we will be open to the voice of the Holy Spirit in our lives. This is true for receiving God's direction and His correction in our lives. It is like studying real money in order to recognize false money when we see it. It is a task of learning the language, culture, customs, and way of a country called heaven so we will recognize the Voice of heaven when He speaks. Let's look at some examples found in the word of God that can help us discern God's voice in our lives.

James 3:17-18 But the wisdom that is from above is first pure, then peaceable, gentle, willing to yield, full of mercy and good fruits, without partiality and without hypocrisy. Now the fruit of righteousness is sown in peace by those who make peace.

When we receive false guidance in our lives we very often become stubborn and defensive in our beliefs. The evidence of our deception is seen in our defensive attitude towards God's direction in our lives. That direction comes from God personally to our hearts, but very often it comes through a voice of authority in the lives of those we are joined to. God wants us to receive His wisdom so we can find the keys to knowing Him. God's wisdom is willing to yield, while self-motivated, self-focused wisdom is defensive and not willing to change. If we are not willing to admit we might be wrong, there is a good chance we are! We may even hear God perfectly, but we may be interpreting what He said in a wrong way. We may be applying what He said wrongly in some way. Every one of us has moments where we become self-focused and defensive towards God's direction in our lives. Our self-will is a carnal will of the flesh. God's will in our lives is an attribute of seeking to give love to God and life to others. These two natures are like that of a wolf versus that which is exhibited in a sheep. I believe that every one of us has the ability to be a sheep and a wolf. When we become self-seeking we manifest the attributes of the wolf. When we become God-seeking we are feeding the sheep nature within us. God wants the sheep nature within us to manifest whereby a life led by the Spirit overpowers the carnal nature of the flesh. This character change within us is even more important than merely making good decisions. It is an attribute of being a son or daughter of God.

We must all remain teachable and humble before God in order to receive His direction in our lives, even when we become distracted by our own agendas. We need to subject what we think God is saying to what He has said in other places and to other people in the past. The Scripture is a true witness to the character, nature, way, power, and authority of God. It is a witness to what He is like so we will not fall for some other influence in our pursuit of life.

The voice of God in our lives includes the process of God's training in our lives. God wants us to know who He is more than He wants us to always have the right answers when we need them. He wants us to have an intimate relationship with Him more than He wants to help us make good decisions in life. There is a training process in knowing the voice of God. That training process involves the voice of God's correction at times. Correction is simply a tool that keeps us in the path of life. It is not a matter of right and wrong, but one of discerning the voice of life and staying in the path of life.

Luke 6:40 "A disciple is not above his teacher, but everyone who is perfectly trained will be like his teacher."

Our example is that of Jesus Christ. He learned obedience through the things He suffered (Heb. 5:8). He was obedient, even unto the cross. That cross was the place of losing His life for the sake of the lives of others. Through that will He has been given a name that is above all other names and has become the inheritor of the nations of the world (Phil. 2:9).

Proverbs 16:22 Understanding is a wellspring of life to him who has it. But the correction of fools is folly.

When we reject God's correction in our lives we become foolish in our ways. Correction is a blessing and not a curse. When we become defensive in our attitude it is many times our own foolish rejection of God's correction in our lives. God corrects us because He loves us. His correction is not a thing of shame, but a willingness on God's part to keep us in the path of life. Let's all be open to God's correction and see the fruit of His righteousness made known in our lives.

Chapter 3

The Process of God's Guidance

There are several elements involved in the process of God's guidance in our lives. We live on every word that comes from the mouth of God. We don't live upon mere information that comes from Him. We live on a personal relationship with Him, whereby He speaks to our hearts from within. God is speaking to us daily that we might know Him and His direction in our lives. To understand God's word in our lives we must first understand that the word of God was never intended to be merely a book. It was perfectly revealed through a person in the flesh of Jesus Christ. When we seek to know God's word we are really seeking to know the person of Christ. We cannot approach hearing God or receiving guidance from Him as mere information by which we can be directed to live. We must approach Him with an aim of knowing who He is in an intimate relationship of life. Even when we read the Scriptures, we are not looking for instructions to live by. We are seeking to know the person God! When we know Him we become empowered to know who we are. When we know who we really are we become empowered to do the things we should do. When we know who we are we become empowered to know how to act in life.

Any word from God is a confirmation of the heart of God revealed in the written word of God. Any word from God must confirm the person of God; it cannot be merely an instruction that confirms us. We are not looking for instructions from God to empower us to live. We are seeking an intimate relationship with God to know Him. He is the one who makes us come alive, not His written word. His written word only serves to activate His living voice within our hearts. The Scripture is a written account of the person God. He is the same yesterday, today, and forever. God is not defined by our personal perceptions of who He is. He simply is, and it is our responsibility to discover who He is. His voice today is not going to contradict His voice in the past. Who He is today is revealed in the testimony of who He has been in the past.

If we are going to be people who hear God and discern His direction in our lives, we must become students of God's word. God as a person will confirm any word He speaks and any expression of His person in the words inspired by Him in the past. Scripture is a written account of the person God, so we must subject any thoughts or directions that come to who God is in His written word. We don't measure Him by the mere accuracy of the written words, but also by the fruit of the Holy Spirit in those words. We must look to understand any expression of God through the fruit of the character of God. He is the same yesterday, today, and forever. When we receive a word from Him we must also see that word confirmed in the will and way of that word in our lives. These three things are known as a revelation from God (word), the interpretation of that word (will), and the application of that word in our lives (way). The Holy Spirit will help us in the process of all three of these and He will submit Himself to the principles, patterns, and values of the written word of God in this process. His present message in our lives will never contradict the principles, patterns, or values found in the written testimony of Him in the past. We don't apply Scripture by fact. We apply Scripture by principle, pattern, and value. The Scripture is not our teacher, the Holy Spirit is, but the Holy Spirit is the one who inspired the Scriptures to be written. The Holy Spirit submits Himself to the word of God because His message will never be different than the word. The understanding of Scripture is subject to the Holy Spirit and the Holy Spirit is subject to the word as it has been expressed revealing who God is.

When reading the written word of God we must always seek to understand what the Holy Spirit was saying to specific people at the time of its written inscription. To be Scripture it had to be relevant at the moment it was given. To be Scripture it had to have been relevant at the moment it was given for doctrine (way of life), reproof, correction, and training in righteousness.

We must also seek to understand what is written in the full language of God. God is not limited in His speech, but we are limited in our understanding. God has used the language of creation, culture, and natural experiences of the world to communicate to us in the word of Scripture. Numbers, symbols, names, idioms, metaphors, elements of creation, and the like are all meant to reveal a continuity of God's covenant language to mankind. What does the Scripture mean in the full language of God? What are its phrases, symbolisms, and concepts in the synthesis of Scripture? What it means in one place carries continuity to all places when applied in the context of its exegetical truth. God is the same yesterday, today, and tomorrow and He wants to communicate with man.

Our final approach to Scripture is to ask, "How does this Scripture apply in my life? How does it change my way of life, reprove me, correct me, or train me in a right relationship with God so that I am equipped for every good work?" The application of Scripture is always by principle, pattern, and value – not by fact. Applying Scripture by 'fact' will cause us to make Scripture of private interpretation (2 Pet. 1:20).

All of these things serve the purpose of knowing whom God is, not merely knowing what to do in life. We must seek to know God as a person in what we discern to be His voice in the present, and subject that voice to what He has revealed to us of Himself in His expressions of the past. These two will agree and will confirm the voice of God in our lives. We can trust His true voice more than we can trust our uneducated, untrained, or misdirected understanding of who He is based upon the imaginations of our own hearts and minds. Being taught by Him will enable us to hear Him clearly and grow in knowing Him in all things. We cannot be lazy. We must be diligent to prove ourselves as workman who need not be ashamed (2 Tim.2:15).

God's guidance in our lives is an issue of intimacy with God. It is like a dance of God's love that leads us into the future realities of His mercy and grace. It is a mystery of faith and a mystery of the Spirit, not simply something easily understood by those bound to natural reasoning or immediate understanding. This means that things around us and things in life will not necessarily seem as though they match God's direction in our lives for the day. This journey with God is one of faith, trust, and most of all intimacy of love with God as our Father and friend.

What About Circumstances?

In my many years as a believer in Christ and as a leader in the body of Christ, I have seen many people substitute circumstantial guidance for intimacy with God. I have seen believers put more confidence in convenient or seemingly confirming circumstances than in trusting their personal relationship with God or even God appointed authority in their lives when it comes to receiving guidance from God. They believe they are looking for an effective door of direction, but they are very often simply looking for the easy way forward in what they believe or hope to be the will of God. Some even present this type of witness as a fleece, such as the fleece of Gideon.

Judges 6:36-40 So Gideon said to God, "If You will save Israel by my hand as You have said— look, I shall put a fleece of wool on the threshing floor; if there is dew on the fleece only, and it is dry on all the ground, then I shall know that You will save Israel by my hand, as You have said." And it was so. When he rose early the next morning and squeezed the fleece together, he wrung the dew out of the fleece, a bowlful of water. Then Gideon said to God, "Do not be angry with me, but let me speak just once more: Let me test, I pray, just once more with the fleece; let it now be dry only on the fleece, but on all the ground let there be dew." And God did so that night. It was dry on the fleece only, but there was dew on all the ground.

Let me point out that Gideon was acknowledging that God had already spoken to Him at his request of a supernatural sign from God. He wasn't looking for a 'first voice' in the matter. He already had faith, he was simply declaring a greater testimony of His faith. He wasn't looking for a sign to give Him faith; he was requesting a sign to strengthen His faith.

The fleece example of Gideon was a super-natural event, not just an arrangement of circumstances. The fleece was wet with dew one day and the ground was kept supernaturally dry, while the fleece was kept supernaturally dry on the second day and the ground was wet with dew. It wasn't just an event of seeing a yellow Volkswagen car in the next hour if God wanted him to go this direction. It wasn't just an eagle flying over his head that confirmed that God wanted him to do a certain thing. It wasn't even seeing the number 7 seven times in seven hours. It was something beyond potentially manipulated or imagined circumstances. Let me also point out the fleece was also given to an Old Covenant man in an Old Covenant time as a confirmation of direction. The fleece was also a one-time event.

I am not saying that God cannot or will not use circumstance to confirm His direction in our lives. I have seen circumstances confirm God's voice many times. What I am saying is that circumstances, or even things like fleeces, are a weaker confirmation to the voice of God than the inner peace and faith that comes by the Holy Spirit.

I have had many times where God has spoken to me and the circumstances were not favorable to indicate any confirmation that I had heard God. Many times circumstances have resisted the will of God in my life. I would say that I have seen more circumstances oppose the voice of God in my life than have immediately confirmed it. We should never take circumstances as a first witness to the voice of God in our lives. When we do see circumstances play in the role of God's direction we must also have other confirming witnesses. The apostle Paul suffered chains, but he said the word of God was not chained (2 Tim. 2:9). We must very often stand in the midst of circumstances to find God's perfect guidance in our lives. Circumstances with the peace of God can lead to the will of God, but circumstances alone are not a good indicator of whether God is leading us a certain way or not. When circumstances are used as a witness in hearing God we must also have God's peace and God's word present in our lives. This includes a confirmation of principal, pattern, and value found in God's written word, because God's written word is a confirmation to the character, nature, way, power, and authority of who God is. Circumstances must also include a release in our hearts. We must never be circumstantially sensitive or bound. We cannot let circumstances sway us from what God has spoken to us nor manipulate us into thinking God has said something when He has not. We cannot allow resisting circumstances to prevent us from responding to God's true guidance and direction in our lives. Many people become discouraged and even swayed in being led by God's Spirit because of circumstances. Unfavorable circumstances don't necessarily mean that we are out of the will of God. Favorable circumstances don't mean we are in the will of God either. If we think that circumstances are a good way of discerning the voice of God, the devil will be sure to give us all the necessary circumstances to lead us astray in our journey with God. Any natural or supernatural signs in our lives must be confirmed by God's intimate voice in our hearts. Depending upon circumstances alone as a witness can cause us to misinterpret the voice of God in the mixed up emotions of our souls. The fruit of the Spirit, the keeping of covenants, a love for God, and a love for others, are stronger witnesses than the witness of circumstances in our lives. A check in your spirit, a break in peace, is a more powerful tool than circumstances. The enemy cannot counterfeit the inner peace of the human heart, but he can manipulate circumstances and even manipulate supernatural things at times.

Deuteronomy 13:1-4 "If there arises among you a prophet or a dreamer of dreams, and he gives you a sign or a wonder, and the sign or the wonder comes to pass, of which he spoke to you, saying, 'Let us go after other gods'—which you have not known—'and let us serve them,' you shall not listen to the words of that prophet or that dreamer of dreams, for the LORD your God is testing you to know whether you love the LORD your God with all your heart and with all your soul. You shall walk after the LORD your God and fear Him, and keep His commandments and obey His voice; you shall serve Him and hold fast to Him.

The enemy doesn't simply show up in your life and tell you to serve some other god than the one you know. He tries to manipulate you into thinking you are serving the God you know through a focus on something that God might do or He could do. If we make circumstances, works, things, or events a goal in receiving God's guidance in our lives, we are setting ourselves up for deception. Hearing God is about an intimate relationship with God. God would rather have us fail in some moment of guidance in our lives, than fail in our love for Him. God does not test us to see us fail, He has given us a free will however, and He wants us to know the supernatural magic of loving Him above all else. If we fail in a journey of His guidance in our lives we can only hope to discover the stronger miracle of learning to love Him above all else in the next chapter of our journey in life. Our love for Him can be stronger than manipulating or controlling circumstances in life.

Knowing the Peace of God

When it comes to hearing God I believe that one of the best witnesses that we have is the peace of God in our own hearts. It is a peace that surpasses the understanding of our minds. We can have conflict in our souls, but peace in our hearts is a sure witness to the voice of God when He speaks to our hearts.

What does it mean to not have peace in a matter? When we feel a hesitation or a 'check' in our spirits it is a caution to peace. Peace is not the absence of conflict in life or in any situation of our lives. Peace is where there is no gap between God and us. This includes no gap between our spirits and His Holy Spirit. The blood of Jesus was the price that gives us full access to the throne of God's grace. There is no gap between God and man if we choose to boldly come before His throne of grace. When we seek God in a matter, or move in the direction of what we believe to be the voice of God within us, we can be assured that Holy Spirit in our hearts will give a clear witness as to the direction we should go. This is confirmed by an inner peace that tells us it is the way to go. When we turn to go in a direction not being guided by God, Holy Spirit is faithful to put a hesitation in our own human spirit. The enemy cannot counterfeit the peace of God in our hearts. Peace occurs when we have a conscious rest or assurance in our hearts concerning a matter. A 'check' in that peace is a sure witness to God redirecting us into the direction of peace when we trust Him. A 'check' in that peace may be a no to the direction we are going, but it may also simply be a yes in another way. We may well have heard God in a word from Him, but we may not yet have a yes in the what, the way, the when, or the how of that word. In any case, when we have a check in the peace in our hearts we need to seek for further witnesses to the direction we sense God is leading us.

Isaiah 26:3 You will keep him in perfect peace, whose mind is stayed on You, because he trusts in You.

The peace of God is not the absence of motion, conflict, or struggle around us. It is the absence of disturbance in our hearts. We can be emotionally stressed, but still have the peace of God in our hearts concerning His will. This was true for Jesus in the Garden of Gethsemane. His soul was in conflict, but His heart was kept in the perfect peace of the Father's will. We must never confuse peace in our emotions with peace in our spirits. Jesus was ready for the will of His Father, because He had peace in His heart. The Spirit within Him was indeed willing!

Matthew 26:38-42 Then He said to them, "My soul is exceedingly sorrowful, even to death. Stay here and watch with Me." He went a little farther and fell on His face, and prayed, saying, "O My Father, if it is possible, let this cup pass from Me; nevertheless, not as I will, but as You will." Then He came to the disciples and found them sleeping, and said to Peter, "What! Could you not watch with Me one hour? Watch and pray, lest you enter into temptation. The spirit indeed is willing, but the flesh is weak." Again, a second time, He went away and prayed, saying, "O My Father, if this cup cannot pass away from Me unless I drink it, Your will be done."

The peace of God in our hearts is not dependent upon good or bad circumstances. It is a state of being that originates within us. It originates within us because it comes from the Holy Spirit within us. It is not conscience. It is beyond conscience. It is the peace of God that floods our spirit and then touches our soul from within. God is the source, not self. It is a peace of God from the inside out, not a voice of peace to our minds from an external input or external observation. The witness of God's peace in our hearts goes beyond our human understanding. It is a knowing within that all is moving in the direction of life.

The peace of God cannot be ours unless we have also made peace with God. The blood of Jesus was enough to give us access to the throne of God's grace. His mercy gives us entrance, but we must choose to pursue access to God's peace in our lives. We must loose on earth what has been authorized to be loosed in heaven. Forgiveness has been loosed for us in heaven, but we must choose to forgive on earth to unlock the blessing of forgiveness in heaven. If we want rain, vapors of water must ascend from the earth to the heavens where the loosing of rain has been established. What is loosed on earth is then loosed from heaven. Angels don't come from heaven. They come from the house of God upon the earth. They ascend from the gate of heaven upon the earth and descend from heaven back to the gate of heaven upon the earth. When angels ascend, they can then return with the blessings of heaven from the storehouses of heaven. This is why they ascended the ladder in Jacob's dream (Gen. 28:12) and this is why they descended upon the Son of man, Jesus Christ, in His ministry of life to the lost sheep of Israel (Jn. 1:51). Each of us must live a life that looses God's peace in order to access God's peace in heaven. Our actions, behavior, and attitudes affect our peace with God. It is not that God takes His peace from us; we choose to remove ourselves from the place of God's true peace when we fail to position ourselves to receive His peace. We end up living some place where grace cannot abide.

Obedience to the voice of God will bring the peace of God in our lives. If we fail to respond to God's voice in our lives we move away from the place of God's peace in our lives. We can't rob a bank, abuse our loved ones, hate our brother, and live selfishly, and expect to experience the peace of God in our hearts! We must embrace the life of God's Spirit and destroy the things in our lives that cause a gap between God and us in order to experience the peace that God wants us to have. Peace with God brings about the peace of God in our lives (Num. 25).

Satan can imitate the voice of God. He can speak through prophecy, signs, visions, dreams, and revelations (Deut. 13:1-3). He can even counterfeit love and goodness and appear as an angel of light. But he cannot imitate the peace of God. When Jesus walks into the room there is peace. This was true of His resurrected presence in the midst of His disciples. They were hiding for fear, but He walked into the room and brought them peace. Before he gave them any instruction he gave them peace.

John 20:19-21 Then, the same day at evening, being the first day of the week, when the doors were shut where the disciples were assembled, for fear of the Jews, Jesus came and stood in the midst, and said to them, "Peace be with you." When He had said this, He showed them His hands and His side. Then the disciples were glad when they saw the Lord. So Jesus said to them again, "Peace to you! As the Father has sent Me, I also send you."

Something happened in the room when Jesus spoke those words. When Jesus walks into the room He gives peace. With every true revelation of or from Him there is peace. If there is no peace, there is no true testimony of Him.

Does the peace of God ever change in our lives? Peace can change because we must have peace for a word from God, the perfect will of that word, and the way that word is to come to pass. We can have peace for something being a word from God, yet still we must wait for the peace of God in our hearts for it being the will of God for us in our lives at this time in our lives. We can have peace for something being a word from God and the will of God in our lives, but we must also discover the peace of God in our hearts for the way of that word. There is a perfect timing, place, and how of happening for any word from God. The peace of God is once again like a dance in our hearts in the guidance of God in our lives. We must learn to listen to the peace of God in our hearts as we move forward in walking out God's way in our lives.

God's voice leads by inspiring our hearts, while Satan is forceful in his attempt to control us and make us respond through some attribute of guilt, shame, or condemnation. There is a spirit of panic and demanded response in his voice. God can be bold, but He always leads. He can induce to activate, but He doesn't drive or push. The voice of God always comes as a voice behind us. A voice behind us is a voice of faith. God's voice is a motivating voice of faith in our hearts.

God wants us to live life with a fresh appointment for living in every moment of our journey. Hearing God is important for a new beginning of every day. Without hearing God we are bound to things we have seen, heard, or thought before. Our souls do not instantly see, hear, or think the things that God has prepared for us, but His Spirit is willing to reveal them to us from within. It is from our spirits that we hear God and then we can know the steps of His wisdom in our lives. If we cannot hear God we are bound to repeat the things of our past.

1 Corinthians 2:9, 10 But as it is written: "Eye has not seen, nor ear heard, nor have entered into the heart of man the things which God has prepared for those who love Him." But God has revealed them to us through His Spirit. For the Spirit searches all things, yes, the deep things of God.

Chapter 4

The Importance of Hearing

For us to have a new beginning every day we have to hear what the Spirit is saying. Hearing God is not an effort of the flesh, but a response to the Spirit. Both Jesus in the gospels and the Holy Spirit in the book of Revelation declared, "He who has an ear to hear, let him hear." Hearing is a response to the Spirit, not a strain of human effort. Hearing God should be easy, but we also hear many other things. This makes hearing God more complicated. We live in a time where we see and hear many things everyday. The rate that information is being made available to our souls is at an all time high. We have audio, video, and cyber space transmissions influencing our lives at an all-time high and at a record rate of speed. In all of this, we see and hear things that influence us with some form of darkness or death in a major way. The daily news is more about reports of the influence of death in people's lives than it is about the life-giving, miraculous things of God in the world.

Although we live in a world where the influence of darkness seems to be at an all-time high, the influence of heaven is also at an all-time high. People are coming to life in Christ all around the world at increasing levels. People are hearing God! The true evidence of hearing God is not merely in His words coming to us, but in a response inspired by those words. The true evidence of hearing someone is seen in our responses to them. When we truly hear God we respond to what He says. Truly hearing God is essential for establishing a sure foundation in our lives that empowers us for everything that comes our way in life.

Luke 6:46-49 "But why do you call Me 'Lord, Lord,' and do not do the things which I say? Whoever comes to Me, and hears My sayings and does them, I will show you whom he is like: He is like a man building a house, who dug deep and laid the foundation on the rock. And when the flood arose, the stream beat vehemently against that house, and could not shake it, for it was founded on the rock. But he who heard and did nothing is like a man who built a house on the earth without a foundation, against which the stream beat vehemently; and immediately it fell. And the ruin of that house was great."

Walking in God's guidance in our lives involves hearing Him and responding to what He says. When we respond to what He says we remove the lifeless things that He has not spoken to us in our lives. We remove the lifeless things, like digging in the sand with a shovel until we reach solid rock for the foundation of our lives. That solid rock is an intimate relationship with God in Christ. Hearing God is not about simply knowing what to do, but it is knowing God. The solid foundation for our lives is in knowing God in every situation of our lives. When we know Him, we can stand in any storm of life. Things of life are going to come against us, but knowing God will empower us to stand in all things. Without hearing God we cannot truly know who He is and without hearing God we cannot follow Him in life.

The gates of hell want to prevail against us in life. Those gates are representative of influences of death and destruction in the lives of humanity. The word 'hell' is a Latin compilation of many words. There are many aspects to hell. It is the realm of the dead (Sheol, Hades, the Grave), a place of all consuming fire (Gehenna), a confining place for spirits of rebellion (Tartaroo, 2 Pet. 2:4), and a place of binding authority (the Bottomless Pit, Rev. 20:1 & 3). We often think of these things in regard to the world that follows the one we know, but there are aspects of these dimensions of hell in this life. Many people live in the realm of the dead. They live in circumstances and environments that rob them of life and they are in need of an invasion of the life of heaven in their everyday earthly realities. Many people live for their present comfort and show no concern for the generations of the future. They, like the children of Israel after Solomon's breach in wisdom before God

(1 Kin. 10 & 11), end up sacrificing the future generations in the fires of selfishness and idolatry. This is even as it was in Ge Hinnom (the valley of Hinnom), when Israel sacrificed the children in the garbage dump to the gods of fire (2 Chr. 28:3; 33:6; Jer. 7:31; 19:2-6).

Jesus came to bring life to those who were dead in this world, not just the dead beyond this present realm. His words to the Pharisees confirmed that the living were both in this world and in that which is to come, as are the dead.

John 5:24-27 "Most assuredly, I say to you, he who hears My word and believes in Him who sent Me has everlasting life, and shall not come into judgment, but has passed from death into life. Most assuredly, I say to you, the hour is coming, and now is, when the dead will hear the voice of the Son of God; and those who hear will live. For as the Father has life in Himself, so He has granted the Son to have life in Himself, and has given Him authority to execute judgment also, because He is the Son of Man."

Mark 12: 26-27 "But concerning the dead, that they rise, have you not read in the book of Moses, in the burning bush passage, how God spoke to him, saying, 'I am the God of Abraham, the God of Isaac, and the God of Jacob'? He is not the God of the dead, but the God of the living. You are therefore greatly mistaken."

The living are those who know God. They are those who have a personal relationship with Him that comes by faith. They hear Him and respond to Him with a personal relationship of intimacy. When we hear God we come alive in Him. When Christ died it confirmed that all died, that all might hear Him and live in this world in the testimony of that which is to come.

2 Corinthians 5:14-15 For the love of Christ compels us, because we judge thus: that if One died for all, then all died; and He died for all, that those who live should live no longer for themselves, but for Him who died for them and rose again.

When we know the voice of God in our daily lives, we can influence the world with the life that comes from knowing Him. The influences of the past can be changed by the greater influence of Christ in us, the hope of glory!

Overcoming the Gates of Hell

God wants each of us to know Him in a very personal way. He wants to give us His grace whereby we can partner with Him in life. When we partner with God we can change the world we live in. As I stated, we live in a world that has many influences of hell. Hell has many gates of influence in the earth and God wants us to be people who bring His life to every place of death around us. The gate of heaven in the human heart is more powerful than the gates of hell in the world.

There was a time when Jesus asked His disciples to define who people said He was. They told him that many people thought He was a reincarnated prophet of the past. He then asked them who they thought He was and Peter answered with words of revelation.

Matthew 16:13-19 When Jesus came into the region of Caesarea Philippi, He asked His disciples, saying, "Who do men say that I, the Son of Man, am?" So they said, "Some say John the Baptist, some Elijah, and others Jeremiah or one of the prophets." He said to them, "But who do you say that I am?" And Simon Peter answered and said, "You are the Christ, the Son of the living God." Jesus answered and said to him, "Blessed are you, Simon Bar-Jonah, for flesh and blood has not revealed this to you, but My Father who is in heaven. And I also say to you that you are Peter, and on this rock I will build My church, and the gates of Hades shall not prevail against it. And I will give you the keys of the kingdom of heaven, and whatever you bind on earth will be bound in heaven, and whatever you loose on earth will be loosed in heaven."

In these verses we see that Jesus referred to Peter as Simon Bar-

Jonah. This was Peter's natural name, defining his natural genealogy. I also believe it was a testimony of who Peter was destined to be and a symbol to whom we are destined to be as children of God. The name Simon means *one who bends like a reed* or *one who hears*. A willingness to bend is a willingness to hear. It can be a weakness or strength. Surely Peter was willing to bend when he denied Jesus three times at the crucifixion, but Peter was also willing to look past the prophets of the past and see who God was in the present. He was able to hear the voice of God the Father in defining Jesus as the Christ, the Son of the living God. The term 'bar-Jonah' defines that Peter was the son (bar) of Jonah. I believe there is a spiritual significance in this term as well. The name Jonah means *dove*. The dove is a symbol of the Holy Spirit. Peter was hearing God as a son of the Holy Spirit. This was the spirit of revelation that comes by hearing God. When Simon Peter heard the voice of the Spirit, Jesus said it was the voice of His heavenly Father speaking to him. He then defined Simon Peter as Peter, a name meaning *little rock* (the Greek word *petros*), but Jesus said that upon this *huge rock* (the Greek word *petra*) Christ would build His church and the gates of hades (the realm of the dead) would not prevail against it. I believe that huge rock was that of being a child of God in Christ that hears the voice of God. I believe it was not just knowing that Jesus was the Christ, but also being part of Christ through an intimate relationship with God. Jesus said that this is what would build His church. The Greek word for church is the world *ekklēsia*. It is a political term used in the common Greek language of that day. If you were to make a governmental decision you would call a quorum, a gathering of needed community members to make a community decision. Jesus was saying that hearing the voice of God as our Father was enough to overcome any influence of hell. When two or three people come together in the name of Jesus it releases the power of heaven upon the earth (Mt. 18:18-19). That name is the authority of Jesus. Christ revealing Himself to and through us is enough to overcome the gates of hell!

Hearing God empowers us to loose the things on earth as they have been loosed in heaven and see the blessings of that loosing brought back to the earth. Hearing God empowers us to bind things on earth as they have been bound in heaven and see the binding of those things brought back to the earth. We are not just souls saved to go to heaven, but human beings destined to be one in our spirits, souls, and bodies for the sake of God's kingdom influence in the earth. The throne of our lives (soul) is empowered by hearing God in our hearts. The power of the Spirit in our hearts brings Christ's salvation to our souls and releases the testimony of the authority of our lives to the world in which we live — as is implied in the trichotomy of the human design (Rev. 13:2).

It is hearing the voice of God that empowers us to be a part of the governing body of Christ in the earth. The body of Christ is the life-giving womb of God in this world. It is the place of heaven's gate. It is the place of heaven's influence in the earth. Gates of hell are influences of death and they lead people to the place of destruction. Hearing God gives us prevailing power against those gates.

Gates of hell are ruling powers that war against the soul. Faith comes by hearing God and it is our faith that overcomes the influences of the world. The voice of God is a voice to the human heart. The heart is the gate of heaven and it is the only legitimate gate by which to hear God. Hearing God doesn't come to our natural understanding. God speaks to our spirits, not our souls. When we hear God in our spirits it floods our souls with life-giving emotions, life-giving reasoning, life-giving thinking, and a life-giving will to bring life to the world. The ear gate, eye gate, or any external sensory gate will resist the gate of the heart in hearing God clearly. It is only by hearing God that our souls can be empowered to make life-giving decisions for the sake of the Father's purpose in the earth. Hearing God's voice is essential for the salvation of our souls.

1 Peter 1:8-9 ...whom having not seen you love. Though now you do not see Him, yet believing, you rejoice with joy inexpressible and full of glory, receiving the end of your faith--the salvation of your souls.

Chapter 5

How Can We Hear God's Voice?

Hearing God's voice is not complicated. It is simply a matter of knowing God and knowing that God is the source of life for each of us. Jesus likened it unto sheep and a shepherd. God cares for us as a good shepherd cares for his flock of sheep. The shepherd's sheep understand that the shepherd is the voice that leads to provision, protection, and destiny.

John 10:14-16 "I am the good shepherd; and I know My sheep, and am known by My own. As the Father knows Me, even so I know the Father; and I lay down My life for the sheep. And other sheep I have which are not of this fold; them also I must bring, and they will hear My voice; and there will be one flock and one shepherd."

Jesus cares for the sheep because He knows that the sheep are a part of the Father's flock. They were born for the Father's care, the Father's protection, and the Father's destiny. Jesus cares for those who belong to His Father. He doesn't care for us like the care of pets. He cares for us as a flock of destiny. He knows that we will provide wool, milk, cheese, and meat for the nations. Our lives will bring provision, protection, and care for the destiny of others. As a shepherd cares for his flock, Jesus cares for us.

The religious of Jesus's day didn't understand the principle of having a relationship with God. They only understood the works of God and the law of God. They thought that hearing God was a matter of doing the things that God commands. They didn't understand that hearing God is a matter of knowing God. It is a matter of finding the life that God gives to those who know Him. Hearing God is a matter of relationship with God.

John 10:24-28 Then the Jews surrounded Him and said to Him, "How long do You keep us in doubt? If You are the Christ, tell us plainly." Jesus answered them, "I told you, and you do not believe. The works that I do in My Father's name, they bear witness of Me. But you do not believe, because you are not of My sheep, as I said to you. My sheep hear My voice, and I know them, and they follow Me. And I give them eternal life, and they shall never perish; neither shall anyone snatch them out of My hand."

As sheep of God, we hear the voice of God. His voice is a voice of eternal life. He makes us come alive. He makes us know that we are protected. His voice clearly reveals to our hearts that we are cared for, protected, and being led forward in the path of destiny.

To whom has it been given to hear? Does everyone hear God's voice? Are there only certain ones that God singles out to hear His voice? Let's look at another testimony of Jesus and those who hear God's voice. The disciples asked Him a question. They wanted to know why He spoke to the multitudes in parables.

Matthew 13:10-15 And the disciples came and said to Him, "Why do You speak to them in parables?" He answered and said to them, "Because it has been given to you to know the mysteries of the kingdom of heaven, but to them it has not been given. For whoever has, to him more will be given, and he will have abundance; but whoever does not have, even what he has will be taken away from him. Therefore I speak to them in parables, because seeing they do not see, and hearing they do not hear, nor do they understand. And in them the prophecy of Isaiah is fulfilled, which says: 'Hearing you will hear and shall not understand, and seeing you will see and not perceive; for the heart of this people has grown dull. Their ears are hard of hearing, and their eyes they have closed, lest they should see with their eyes and hear with their ears, lest they should understand with their heart and turn, so that I should heal them.' "

When the disciples asked this question of Jesus, I don't believe that they were much different than the multitudes. They heard the same parables that Jesus spoke to the crowd. What was the difference between the multitudes and the disciples? Why was it given to them to understand what Jesus was saying? I don't think that the disciples understood the parables of Jesus anymore than the multitudes did. The difference was that when Jesus walked off, the disciples followed Him. It was when they sat down with Him that He would explain to them the meaning of the parables. A parable is literally a simple story told to reveal some measure of spiritual truth. It is a story about some natural event or situation that is intended to inspire a greater revelation of hidden truth. I believe that God still uses this principle in our lives today. When we first hear Him we don't truly understand Him. He uses words, stories, or situations that inspire our hearts to desire to understand a deeper meaning. I believe that He speaks like this in order to inspire a response of faith. He wants us to walk off with Him and allow Him to give us the understanding of what He says. God wants us to come to faith in our relationship with Him, not just in our understanding of what He is saying to us. He knows that faith is a substance and a conviction of things hoped for. He knows that only faith can change the world we live in (Heb. 11:1-3). Faith comes by hearing God and faith is towards Him as a person, not merely towards a promise that He gives.

I know that all people can hear God, but only some people recognize the importance of truly hearing Him. They are willing to seek a personal relationship with Him and an understanding of His voice in their lives. God is speaking to all people, but only some recognize Him as a shepherd in their lives. Only some walk off with Him to understand the words that He is speaking. It is not a matter of knowing what to do or where to go. It is a matter of knowing Him.

When God first speaks to us we don't really hear Him. We are simply inspired to seek His presence that we might truly hear Him. Hearing God is not merely a means of knowing what to do. It is a thing of intimacy and relationship with God. Hearing God is about knowing God. Hearing God makes us come alive. It makes us come alive to God. Now is the time when people can hear God and live!

John 5:25 "Most assuredly, I say to you, the hour is coming, and now is, when the dead will hear the voice of the Son of God; and those who hear will live."

It is simple. It is a matter of knowing that we live on every word that comes from the mouth of God. When we hear God we come alive inside. His first words to us are a bit of a mystery. They are like parabolic speech. They are words that inspire us to walk off with Jesus to hear Him. Holy Spirit has come in the name of Jesus and He is the voice of God within us that brings us to faith. It is not complicated. It is for all who know that what He first says is only an invitation to walk off with Him to truly hear what He says. It is for those who know that hearing Him is about knowing Him.

Chapter 6

Recognizing God's Voice

1. God is Spirit

What is hearing God's voice? Hearing God's voice is hearing God's words within our hearts. When we hear God, faith happens. Faith is a supernatural experience that floods our hearts when we hear God. Faith is the substance of things hoped for and it is faith that forms the ages of men. When we hear God it gives us a new beginning for a new day. When He speaks life happens and even the most difficult situation can become a testimony revealing His goodness and love. Hearing God is a testimony of knowing who He is. The religious Pharisees of Jesus's day did not hear Him because they did not know Him. They had a relationship with God's written word, but they didn't have a relationship with God. We must not be like the Pharisees. Our love for the written word of God, or our preconceived ideas of what the written word declares, cannot exceed our love for God. Truly hearing God is birthed in a personal relationship with Him.

John 8:47 "He who is of God hears God's words; therefore you do not hear, because you are not of God."

Faith doesn't come from knowing the written word of God. Knowing the written word of God can help us recognize His voice when He speaks, but that is if we seek His word in order to know God. When we seek Him in His word we discover Him in His character, nature, way, power, and authority. We discover the substance of who God truly is in the totality of His written word. Thinking one knows God by mere memorization of Scripture or legalistic adherence to what one believes to be the do's and don'ts of the written word will actually hinder one in hearing God. Hearing is of faith and as I have stated, faith is towards a person and it works through love. The Spirit of God fills our hearts and lives when we hear His voice within. It is a testimony of the miracle of faith that comes by hearing Him.

Romans 10:17 So then faith comes by hearing, and hearing by the word of God.

Hearing the word of God is not about memorizing what He has said in the past. It is not about living by a set of rules set in the words He has spoken. Faith is only found when God personally speaks to our hearts. When we hear Him within it changes everything within us. Our spirits are ignited with life by the power of God's Spirit within. When our hearts come alive by God's voice our souls are renewed. Our will, our imagination, our reasoning, and our emotions become motivated with purpose and a focus for destiny.

Hearing God's voice is essential for the salvation of our souls. The salvation of our souls is not a matter of believing God and then going to heaven when we die. The human soul is the throne of the human life. It is the bridge between the human spirit and the human life. The power of humanity is within the human spirit, the throne of humanity is within the human soul, and the authority of humanity is demonstrated through each human life. God wants the throne of the human life to be one with the throne of heaven. This is how heaven becomes a reality in the lives of humanity. Faith has become devolved in much of our understanding to be a 'belief system'. If faith is a 'belief system', then what is the difference between faith and law? I believe that adhering to Christian principles is the same as adhering to Biblical law. Faith is much more real than that. It is toward the person God and it comes by hearing Him. When we hear Him it brings increasing salvation to the expression of our will, mind, intellect, reasoning, and emotions. The human soul takes on the characteristics of God's Spirit and it is then expressed through the actions of a human life. This is truly the salvation of humanity. It is for now, and it leads to the greater glory of eternity in Christ!

1 Peter 1:8-9 ...whom having not seen you love. Though now you do not see Him, yet believing, you rejoice with joy inexpressible and full of glory, receiving the end of your faith--the salvation of your souls.

The apostle Peter was writing to the scattered Jewish church of the first century. His challenge was for them to find hope in the midst of their adversity. The traditions of the past had ended and very soon the whole religious structure of the past would be destroyed. The faith of the firstfruit church was not based upon traditions established through a New Covenant church structure. Their faith was inspired by the voice of God within their hearts. The wisdom for the moment would come through the voice of God in their hearts. The salvation of their souls was not just a salvation unto heaven but also a salvation for bringing the influence of heaven into their present reality upon the earth.

Religious church history with its rules and regulations has given us a wrong perspective of God's word and hearing Him. We can't just use the Scriptures to hear God. We must open our hearts to His voice so that we can hear Him. It is through a relationship with God that we are able to hear what He says. God's voice will never contradict the principles, patterns, or values found in His written word. His voice will be true to the principles of His truth, but faith doesn't come from His principles. Faith comes by hearing God!

Hearing God is a matter of relationship with Him. We hear Him and then we walk off with Him to understand what it is that He has said to us. God doesn't just want to speak to us plainly; He wants to speak in a way that inspires us to seek Him that we might live. People who merely want God to tell them what to do may never know a testimony of knowing Him. Hearing God is not about doing what God tells us to do. Hearing God is not about understanding what God said. Hearing God is about understanding God's heart and knowing a life-receiving relationship with Him.

John 10:24-28 Then the Jews surrounded Him and said to Him, "How long do You keep us in doubt? If You are the Christ, tell us plainly." Jesus answered them, "I told you, and you do not believe. The works that I do in My Father's name, they bear witness of Me. But you do not believe, because you are not of My sheep, as I said to you. My sheep hear My voice, and I know them, and they follow Me. And I give them eternal life, and they shall never perish; neither shall anyone snatch them out of My hand."

Hearing God is a matter of eternal life, not a matter of merely knowing what to do. I used to fast and pray in order to know what to do, but I have discovered that fasting and praying is really about spending time with Him. I don't pray to receive answers, I pray to Him, I talk with Him, that I might know Him. I find that when I seek to know Him He gives me answers that I need when I need them, but those things are sub categories to what is really important. I don't seek Him for a supernatural experience or an angelic encounter. I seek Him! What is really important is to know God. Days of knowing what to do and days of not knowing what to do are the environmental conditions that can distract us from God or inspire us to know Him. The decision to seek to know Him is found in our hearts.

I used to fast to know answers from Him, but one day I realized that fasting was more about taking time to indulge in God than it was about seeking answers. It is fine to abstain from food to seek God, but the mere abstinence of food is an Old Covenant form of fasting. New Covenant fasting is about taking the time to feast on God's presence and words. It may involve abstaining from food, but the secret is not in the abstinence of food that feeds the flesh, it is found in the eating of food that feeds the human spirit. We live on every word that comes from God. I have learned that when I seek Him, He wants my time to be with Him, not merely seeking answers from Him. Sometimes I ask Him about certain situations or concerns in my life only to discern that He doesn't really want to talk about them when I ask. I have discovered that if I back away from pressing Him on an issue that I can enjoy time simply seeking Him and loving Him. When I spend a week simply loving Him, He gives me answers to my questions, concerns, or situations in dreams, thoughts, and desires that emerge from within my heart. He wants to give me the answers that I need, but He wants me to know Him even more.

Hearing God for right choices makes 'right choices' your God. Hearing God is not about making right choices and right decisions. Those are merely fruit and evidence of the real issue. Hearing God is about life, not right and wrong decisions.

The key to hearing God is the human heart. When we give our hearts to God we can hear Him. The heart is the gate of heaven and it is the proper receiver for hearing God. We don't hear God in our minds, we hear Him in our hearts. Faith comes by hearing Him and faith is an issue of the heart, it is not an issue of the mind. It affects the mind, but it initiates in our hearts. When we hear Him, our minds become filled with thoughts, reasoning, imaginations, emotions and desires, but the source of them all is God's voice within our hearts. God speaks to all of us in a way that inspires our hearts to be given to Him.

We must learn to recognize God's voice. Hearing God is not a strain to hear what He is saying, but an observing to see Him. Where is He? If we recognize where He is we can hang out with Him. This is not some geographical location. It is a relational location. He can be found in some area of our hearts. What is He doing in us? How is He revealing who He is in our hearts? This is where we hear Him.

We must look to see Him wherever He is. We must be hungry to hear Him today and not merely satisfied to know the words that He has spoken to us in the past. I have learned that people in the world often hear Him before the church does. People in the church are often busy trying to live on the words that He has spoken in the past. They are often focused on preserving their past experiences with God. People in the world don't know that they are seeking God, but they are often seeking new experiences in life. They are seeking to live from their hearts and thus their hearts are vulnerable to the voice of God. Because they don't know Him, they most often misinterpret what they hear, but they are hearing something of Him nonetheless. The result is perceptions that sound something like God, but are filtered through a self-centered, self-seeking, self-satisfying mindset. I look at them like secular prophets. They hear God, they just don't understand what He is saying. I have found that in my personal relationship with God, if I look to hear what they are hearing it helps me understand what God is truly saying. People in the church are often resistant to the voice of God in the world, therefore they seek to preserve the past words of God in their lives. They get stuck living from their minds and resist the wildness of living from the heart. Hearing is found only in the heart. We must learn who God is and then we will hear His voice from the freedom of our hearts. We must not be bound or limited by what God has spoken in the past. His words to us in the past may have only been what we were able to hear in the past. He is leading us forward in a path of destiny and we can expect His words to us to go beyond what we could receive or understand yesterday.

A word from God must produce faith. Faith works through love; therefore, faith must be towards a person and not merely a promise. When we hear God, faith happens (Rom. 10:17). Faith is a supernatural substance that happens when we hear God. God's words to our hearts are faith-filled and they are fear-empty. God's words to our hearts are expressions of His love and His perfect love casts out all fear.

God doesn't want to control or manipulate us to do things. The voice of the Lord is a voice behind us (Rev. 1:10). When God speaks the substance of faith inspires us to move forward. His voice is not controlling or manipulating, it inspires our hearts to respond to Him. When we are filled with faith we become faithful in all that we do. It is not a matter of working harder, but a matter of believing God in our hearts. To be faithful we must quit working so hard, get intimate with Him, and be a hard worker. Faith removes all doubt from our hearts. It is faith that shows us the path of life and faith comes when we hear God. It is a supernatural power of life that works in our hearts.

Romans 14:23 But he who doubts is condemned if he eats, because he does not eat from faith; for whatever is not from faith is sin.

Whatever is not from faith is sin. Whatever is not from faith is 'missing the mark'. It is missing the connection of life and the connection that leads to life for others. How do we know that what we are hearing is a word from God? To be word it has to be true to what a word from God can be. It must be true to the character, nature, way, power, and authority of God. To be a spoken word from God it has to be the way He speaks. We learn His way through a personal relationship with Him as a person, not as a ruler or commander. Intimacy with God is the key to understanding His heart.

A word from God must be Scriptural in content as well as in Spirit. He is the same yesterday, today, and forever. His character, nature, way, power and authority remain consistent and evident in all that He has said and in all that He says today. Our preconceived ideas and personal prejudices often cause our minds to misinterpret what He has said, but when we allow the Holy Spirit to be the one who gives the true understanding of His truth we increasingly understand His voice. Jesus, the man, was not interpreted through Scripture; the Scripture is only properly translated and understood through a revelation of Jesus. Jesus is the true testimony of the prophetic word of Scripture. The truth of the word, with the fruit of the Spirit, must be present in any word we believe to be from God. God is all about giving, not taking. He doesn't take life from us; He gives life to us. When we believe we are hearing God we must check the motive of our hearts. We must let the Holy Spirit do an examination. Any word from God will inspire our hearts to be seekers of God and others, not seekers of ourselves. Our examination is not one of condemnation, but one of dependency upon God for the sake of bringing life to the world. We must never do an improper examination of the body of Christ. Each of us is a member of His body. If we stay intimate with Him we will hear Him, and His words will be love-motivating, not self-motivating.

We must never go to the Bible with the desire to justify our own desires, but rather submit them to the word of God and have them come in line with the known logos of God. We must take the word of God as we think it to be and submit it to the word of God we know to be.

We must be willing to grow in our understanding of the logos of God in order to grow in our hearing of the rhema of God. This means our understanding of the logos of God will mature and grow according to God's mercy and grace. The rhema of God is His speaking word to our hearts, while the logos of God are His expressions in the past that include His expressions in Scripture. We must be willing to let go of what we think God's word says and be open to the Holy Spirit's maturing process in our lives in understanding what His word truly says. We must put that which is subjective under that which is objective. We must always submit what is being expressed to what has been expressed, but we must allow a revelation of Christ in our hearts to influence our understanding of what God meant through His expressions in the past. Christ in us is the hope of glory, not our personal interpretation of what we believe He meant by what He said or did yesterday. By doing this we will grow in our revelation, interpretation, and application of His words to us. We must always submit what we think He has expressed in the past to the fullness of who He is in all of His expressions, in order to understand what He has said.

We don't clearly understand the words that we hear Him speak. We understand Him clearly when we learn the language that He speaks. A number of years ago I was in the nation of Macedonia. It was my first trip there. I and those with me were left alone with the pastor's brother and his family for about an hour. During our hour together we attempted to have a conversation with the man and his family. When the pastor returned he asked us how we were doing. We said that we had a wonderful conversation with his brother and his family and we thought that we had come to some understanding of what he had said. The pastor asked us what we thought his brother had said. We proceeded to tell him that we understood that his brother had a moderately sized farm with twenty or more milking cows. The actual fact was that his brother had a cow and a small piece of land. We heard the words clearly, but we didn't understand the Macedonian language. This is often the case with God and us. We hear His words clearly, but we don't speak the language of heaven. We must grow in understanding God's language in order to properly interpret and apply what He is saying in our lives.

Many years ago my family and I lived in a two floor, five bedroom log home that I had built in the country. I had put many hours of labor into the project, but during the season of our journey of carving out an earthly dream in the forest I had heard God's call on my life to ministry. One day, while sitting in my office, I heard God speak. He said, "Get everything out of your house that you don't want to burn." I had put many years of effort to build that house with hand-manufactured tools, a chain saw, and material extracted and hewn from the land it stood upon. It was a sacrifice of my own self for something that I loved. During that season I experienced God in a fresh and powerful way. My heart was being impassioned and motivated to pursue a life of serving God. God had changed my love. My heart had now been captured by a love for Him and a love to serve Him by loving people. The house wasn't so important anymore. When God spoke what He did to me, I wasn't sure if the house was going to literally burn down or not. God had spoken to my wife the same day in the same way. It was about a week before we conferred with one another as to what God had spoken to us. Our oldest son also had a dream that an airplane crashed into our house and it burned to the ground. We decided that the family pictures and the important papers were the only things we wanted to keep safe so we moved them to my office in town, in case the house burned down. We put ladders to the second floor and practiced fire drills with our family. When we were out driving around and saw smoke in our direction, we often thought it could be the house burning down. The house never did burn down. We eventually sold it and moved into the city. God's words to us were not about the house burning down, they were about our hearts being changed to love Him more than our visions and dreams of the past. He was changing our hearts to pursue the path that He had for us in ministry. I believe that my son's dream of the airplane crashing into the house and the house burning down was a symbolism of things from heaven becoming more important and powerful than the things of our past. It was time to move forward into all God had for us.

2. A Testimony of Him

When we receive a word that we believe to have come from God we must look to see if the word is true to the character and nature of God. God is not a gossip, so He won't tell us things about others so we can talk bad about them. He doesn't point the finger to sin. He is willing to forgive sin and remember it no more forever, but He is not into spreading shame on others. He won't speak secrets to us so that we can know more secrets than others. His words to us don't make us elite or separate from others. God has secrets so He can tell them. His secrets are not meant to be hidden, but to become revealed mysteries for common understandings of life. It is not about knowledge for the sake of knowledge, but a knowing of Him to enhance our relationship with Him and with others, When He reveals His secrets to us they are meant to belong to our children and our children's children.

Deuteronomy 29:29 "The secret things belong to the LORD our God, but those things which are revealed belong to us and to our children forever, that we may do all the words of this law."

In the terms of the New Covenant and grace, the secrets of God are revealed to us that we might become who we need to be. This is not just for us, but also for the sake of our unfolding inheritance in the earth. If we have more secrets than what we can say, maybe we are living in the wrong house. The Holy Spirit's gift of suspicion with the corresponding fruit of criticism and judgment is not a true reality of Christ. These are not attributes of the Holy Spirit. Any word given to us by God must result in life-giving words to others. The sword of the Spirit is not the logos of God, it is the rhema. The sword of the spirit is not the Bible; it is God's life-giving words being expressed though our lives to others. It is the testimony of loving God and loving others.

Ephesians 6:17b ... and the sword of the Spirit, which is the word of God...

The word for 'word' in this verse is not the Greek logos, but the Greek rhema. It is God speaking to us now which causes us to become expressions of Him to others. This is always a matter of giving life and not a matter of judgment, law, or right and wrong measuring. God doesn't just want us to know what He has said; He wants us to hear what He is saying. His words to us are given to cause us to become a testimony of life to the world.

What is the true test of knowing whether a word is from God or not? John wrote that the true testimony is within us. It is the anointing within us that teaches us.

1 John 4:1-3 Beloved, do not believe every spirit, but test the spirits, whether they are of God; because many false prophets have gone out into the world. By this you know the Spirit of God: Every spirit that confesses that Jesus Christ has come in the flesh is of God, and every spirit that does not confess that Jesus Christ has come in the flesh is not of God. And this is the spirit of the Antichrist, which you have heard was coming, and is now already in the world.

The Greek word for 'has come' is in the perfect and imperfect tense. This means it is something that has happened, is continuing to happen, and will continue to happen. It is not in the aorist tense, meaning an event from the past. Jesus came in the flesh 2000 years ago, but the test of a word from God is not a belief that Jesus simply came in history. The devil has no problem with Jesus coming in the flesh 2000 years ago. His real problem is Christ in you. The Spirit that says Christ has come in your flesh is of God. The witness is within the believer.

This is the true witness to the voice of God in our lives. It is the anointing of Christ within us that bears witness to the voice of God to us. I grew up in a Lutheran church, because my family was of the Lutheran faith. I believed that Jesus came in the flesh as a man, but He had not yet come into my flesh. There were times when I can remember the touch of God's Spirit in my life, but there was no conception of God's Spirit in my heart. I believed the word of God to a degree, but I didn't understand it much since there was no true witness of God's voice in my heart. When I received the witness of Christ within me everything changed. I now had a witness to the words of God to me by the presence of Christ within me. Any word from God will bear witness with the presence of Christ in me. This is the true test of a word being from God. We have an anointing within us that teaches us.

1 John 4:4 You are of God, little children, and have overcome them, because He who is in you is greater than he who is in the world.

1 John 2:20 But you have an anointing from the Holy One, and you know all things.

1 John 2:27 But the anointing which you have received from Him abides in you, and you do not need that anyone teach you; but as the same anointing teaches you concerning all things, and is true, and is not a lie, and just as it has taught you, you will abide in Him.

The Holy Spirit will never tell us to do something contrary to the nature of God or Scripture. This is not our preconceived ideas concerning God's nature or the meaning of Scripture. It is who God is. Sex outside of the covenant of marriage is a destructive force of dysfunction and death, even if two people love each other. This is why the Scripture sets this boundary. It is not about being wrong, but a matter of dysfunction and death. God doesn't want this to be a law of accountability that we live by. He wants it to be a value and understanding in our hearts. We cannot light fire where fire is not supposed to burn. When someone ignites an illegitimate flame in their hearts it doesn't matter what you say to them. You cannot counsel people when a wrong fire is burning, because the flames consume all that you say. We must learn the boundaries of life and then seek to walk in those boundaries to find true life. It is not a matter of law; it is a matter of finding life in the place where life abides. It is a matter of living in a personal relationship with God and living on the words of His heart.

We must expose every thought, impression, and suggestion that comes from any source, to God's word. We must submit them to the whole Bible regardless of how spiritual or religious they may sound. We are not looking to confirm a word by the legalism of Scripture. We are looking for the person Christ in the character, nature, way, power and authority of the words that we hear.

2 Corinthians 10:3-6 For though we walk in the flesh, we do not war according to the flesh. For the weapons of our warfare are not carnal but mighty in God for pulling down strongholds, casting down arguments and every high thing that exalts itself against the knowledge of God, bringing every thought into captivity to the obedience of Christ, and being ready to punish all disobedience when your obedience is fulfilled.

The knowledge of God is not knowledge about God. It is an intimate knowing of Him. When we know Him we understand His character, nature, way, power, and authority. If we heard a thought to rob a bank we would know that it is not the voice of God. If we heard a thought to murder someone we would know that it is not the voice of God. If we hear a thought to commit adultery we should know that it is not the voice of God. These thoughts don't come so obviously. They are often disguised in the form of taking what belongs to another, harboring unforgiveness or some form of bitterness for another, or seeking to meet our own needs even in some form of compromise. These things are not the nature of God; therefore, they cannot be the voice of God. We must know who God is to hear what He says to us in life.

3. Preparing to Recognize God's Voice

As part of the redeemed human race, we live by the life of Christ within our hearts. It is in that place of intimacy with God that we hear His voice from within. He desires a relationship with us that is based upon His love, not merely His sovereign ability to be God. He wants for us to hear Him so we will know who He is. God is always speaking in our lives, but we are not always listening. He is always communicating with us, but we don't always understand what He is saying. We often don't even realize that it is Him speaking. To recognize God's voice in our lives, we must prepare to recognize it. We must rightly divide His word of truth to us. Paul told Timothy to do so as a leader in the church.

2 Timothy 2:15 Be diligent to present yourself approved to God, a worker who does not need to be ashamed, rightly dividing the word of truth.

To rightly divide God's word we must get down to the spirit of the word. To do this we must choose to study the written word of God to understand the character, nature, way, power, and authority of God's words. We find this by looking at the 'big picture' of Scripture. We must live for the whole story, not just a verse in the story. Jesus said that to be His disciple we must hate our father and mother. This verse by itself is not truth. It is meant to express the strength of loving God, not the option of hating our parents. The Scripture in its entirety teaches us that honoring our fathers and mothers is a huge issue in regard to our love for them and our destiny in life. God doesn't want us to hate our parents. He wants us to know the wonder of His love. Our love for God is so powerful it makes our love for our parents look like hate. Even when we must choose God over our parents we don't do so to hate our parents. We only make those choices based upon our love for God. It is not an excuse to hate our parents, but a passion for loving God.

God's word is not given for us to exalt the spirit, belittle the soul, and hate the flesh. The past expressions of God are keys to activate the present expression of God in our lives each day. We must each allow God's word to unite our soul and our spirit in order to see His word embodied in our lives.

Hebrews 4:12 For the word of God is living and powerful, and sharper than any two-edged sword, piercing even to the division of soul and spirit, and of joints and marrow, and is a discerner of the thoughts and intents of the heart.

This verse is talking about the logos of God. The logos is something expressed by God in the past, such as Scripture. Something that has been expressed by God has the ability to pierce into our hearts and activate the voice of God within us. The word of God allows the life of God's Spirit within us to be drawn into our souls. The word (logos) of

God causes the secret part of us to be drawn into public view.

The Holy Spirit within our hearts will be activated by the true character expressions of the Holy Spirit as they pierce through to our hearts. A right spirit releases a right energy. A wrong spirit releases wrong energy. Christ in us is the hope of glory, not merely Christ to us.

To properly prepare ourselves to hear God we must ask this question concerning what we believe is being said: "Is this word Scriptural and have I talked to God personally about it?" Just because something sounds like Scripture, doesn't mean that it is Scriptural. The devil knows how to quote Scripture, but he cannot speak with a life-giving spirit.

1 Timothy 4:4-5 For every creature of God is good, and nothing is to be refused if it is received with thanksgiving; for it is sanctified by the word of God and prayer.

I don't believe that these verses are talking about praying a prayer at our tables before we eat. This may not be a bad thing to do, but praying over something doesn't make it sanctified. If this was the case we might as well pray like this: "God bless this heroin I'm about to receive. I give You thanks for this bountiful supply." Perhaps we could pray like this: "Father you know my heart. Please bless this adulterous relationship that I am about to enter into. You know how I have longed for the freedom of true relationship." Or maybe a prayer like this: "Thank You Jesus for this dog poop that I am about to eat. Please dull my sense of smell so I can ingest all that has been given to me." "Please show me whether or not You want me to rob this bank." "Please anoint me to grasp for power and despise the authority in our ministry, our business, or our community." These statements may sound foolish, but if we think about it, we have prayed some very ridiculous prayers to justify what we think should be the will of God. For something to be sanctified by the word of God it must first be true to the character of God found in His word. For something to be sanctified by God's word it must be true to something He would say, He must be saying it, and we must have had a face-to-face conversation with Him in the matter.

The word of this verse is the logos of God, something that God has said. The prayer in this verse is the active receiving of His rhema, what He is saying right now to you. Prayer is not a ritual or some form of magical religious words. It is a personal conversation with God in a manner of intimacy. Not all things are meant to be received for personal consumption. Not all places are places to go. Everything has a purpose. A thorny hedge is to keep things out, so don't choose to live in a thorny hedge. Some things in life are meant to be avoided while others are meant to be sought out. Everything has a purpose. Some questions to ask in regard to what we believe God is saying are: "Is it Scriptural and have I talked to God about it?" "Do I have faith to do this?" Faith is a natural response to a supernatural relationship. Faith happens when we hear God speaking to our hearts and it is not simply an emotional desire of our souls.

Chapter 7

Hindrances to Hearing

God loves people and He is speaking to us all the time. He is speaking more than we are listening. We hear God better than we think; the problem is that we hear many other things as well. If we can identify the hindrances to hearing Him, we can then also focus on hearing Him more clearly. God's voice is a voice of the Spirit. It is a voice of faith. The opposite of faith is natural sight. How things look, sound, feel, or are perceived to be in some natural way can be a hindrance to hearing God. God communicates to our spirits by His Holy Spirit. He doesn't speak to our souls; He speaks to our hearts.

1 Corinthians 2:9-16 But as it is written: "Eye has not seen, nor ear heard, nor have entered into the heart of man the things which God has prepared for those who love Him." But God has revealed them to us through His Spirit. For the Spirit searches all things, yes, the deep things of God. For what man knows the things of a man except the spirit of the man which is in him? Even so no one knows the things of God except the Spirit of God. Now we have received, not the spirit of the world, but the Spirit who is from God, that we might know the things that have been freely given to us by God. These things we also speak, not in words which man's wisdom teaches but which the Holy Spirit teaches, comparing spiritual things with spiritual. But the natural man does not receive the things of the Spirit of God, for they are foolishness to him; nor can he know them, because they are spiritually discerned. But he who is spiritual judges all things, yet he himself is rightly judged by no one. For "Who has known the mind of the Lord that he may instruct Him?" But we have the mind of Christ.

In these verses we see that the natural man cannot receive the things of God. This is not merely the carnal, flesh motivated man. It is the natural part of humanity. Each of us has a natural man. Each of us must recognize that we have a natural part of us that hears God, but it doesn't know what God is really saying. This is our natural man. We must learn to submit our natural man to the mind of Christ that is within us. Each of us has a natural man, but Christ in us also gives each of us the mind of Christ. We do not judge the voice of God by our natural understanding. We can only properly discern the voice of God by the quickening of our spirits by the Spirit of Christ within us. We don't judge prophecy by natural understanding, but by the witness of our spirits as God's true voice is quickened by the Spirit of Christ within our hearts. This is how we judge any expression of God's voice to our lives. We discern His voice by that internal witness. Our natural man is part of who we are. It is not a bad thing; it is simply the natural part of us. We must accept that our natural man is good, but it is also a challenge to our ability to hear God. The natural part of us simply makes us dependent upon the spirit part of us. This is how our soul, the bridge between the spirit and the natural being, becomes led by the voice of God.

If we can recognize that our natural man can become a hindrance in our hearing God's voice, we can then allow it to become a strong part of our lives as we allow our souls to be led by the Spirit. Our natural man is supposed to be a visible expression of the spirit man within us. We don't hear God by the outward observations of our lives, but the outward circumstances of our lives should be changed by the power of the voice of God within our hearts. Our ages (worlds) should be framed by faith that comes through God's words in our hearts (Heb. 11:3). We must allow God's voice to empower our natural expressions in life and we must never let the natural realities of our lives become stronger than the voice of God within our hearts. If we take the posture that the first thing that will hinder us from hearing God's voice is human understanding and human wisdom, we will be ready to hear God more clearly. True wisdom is not based on experience. The spirit of Wisdom comes from faith toward God and it is part of the seven-fold expression of the Holy Spirit in our lives. Once something has been expressed in our lives it creates an evidence of the wisdom that was given, but if it becomes a rule or a method to the future it will only serve to give us a future that is limited to our past.

We must embrace understanding God in our hearts more than with our heads. If we allow our heads to become a stronger influence than our hearts, we will be bound to an understanding of the soul based upon how we think naturally, how we reason naturally, and how it feels naturally. Our souls' understanding will affect our ability to hear in the spirit. There is nothing wrong with the soul, but when it is left to itself it becomes a power of self (selfish). When we listen with natural ears or see with natural eyes, our soul will hinder us from hearing God's voice.

The soul is connected to the spirit. The flesh is connected to the soul. When our souls line up with the life within 'Christ in us the hope of glory' becomes a powerful source of life to the natural expressions of our lives. We must see our souls as the thrones of our lives that are led by our spirits within. The Holy Spirit of God in our hearts leads our spirits. We must know the voice of the Creator within our hearts stronger than any outside source of creation. If we seek life from an outside source, we are feeding our souls from an illegitimate life supply.

Each of us hears God through our spirit, not our soul. Our spirits are empowered with the life of Christ within us and our souls prosper according to the life inspired from within. God created the human soul to be inspired by the human spirit. When the human spirit is not empowered by the substance of God's Spirit within, the human soul becomes susceptible to the sway of other spirit influences. We have an adversary who schemes against our soul. Our spirit is the key to our soul hearing God's voice, but our soul is the very key to hearing our spirit. Spiritual powers of wickedness and unrighteousness know our vulnerability. The devil wars against our soul, not our spirit. His strategy is to get human beings to be led by their own fleshly desires, rather than the life of God within them.

1 Peter 2:11 Beloved, I beg you as sojourners and pilgrims, abstain from fleshly lusts which war against the soul...

Ephesians 6:12 For we do not wrestle against flesh and blood, but against principalities, against powers, against the rulers of the darkness of this age, against spiritual hosts of wickedness in the heavenly places.

The enemy attempts to get us to draw our life (soul supply) from an outside source. High places are the key to principalities. False spirits and lies create strongholds of beliefs in human hearts. Those beliefs inspire actions. Those actions activate the power of creative thoughts. Those creative thoughts transpire to become influences, expressed in various forms, that affect the thinking and even the lives of others. Beliefs are often expressed as attitudes. Those attitudes become revealed through actions in our lives.

Those actions craft expressions, and even scribe epitaphs, of what we believe in our own imaginations and in the inheritance we pass on to others. Those actions then become the foundation for further imaginations that even become inheritances to be received by others through our influence in the world. We must stand in intimacy with God in the Spirit to see the beliefs of our hearts transformed and the influences of our lives changed. The beliefs of our hearts are the key to either hearing the voice of God in our hearts or the voice of an enemy through our souls.

A devil wars against the human soul in an attempt to infiltrate the belief of the human heart. His voice is a voice that comes to us from the outside. It is a voice that seeks to penetrate our thoughts, our imaginations, our reasoning, our emotions, and even our wills through repetitious patterns, seductive invitations, traumatic experiences, or some other device that seeks to crack or penetrate our souls. The devil tempts us to make a trade in our identity. He wants to crack our souls and trick us to believe that his personality is our personality. A spirit of fear is afraid and it schemes to crack the human soul and convince the person to receive that spirit of fear and become fearful. It is through the soul that the enemy seeks to penetrate our hearts. It is a matter of yielding our wills to the will of a foreign spirit. To make this happen the enemy will use our own desires against us. How is the enemy able to cause our own desires to war against our souls?

James 1:13-15 Let no one say when he is tempted, "I am tempted by God"; for God cannot be tempted by evil, nor does He Himself tempt anyone. But each one is tempted when he is drawn away by his own desires and enticed. Then, when desire has conceived, it gives birth to sin; and sin, when it is full-grown, brings forth death."

God will test our faith because He wants us to know His voice. God is not the one who tempts us, but God is the one who allows us to be tested. His voice is a voice inside our hearts. It is a voice of intimacy with Him in our spirits. We hear Him in our spirits and then our spirits flood our souls to convey His voice to our souls. God knows that our true strength comes from His voice inside our hearts, thus He is not afraid of the enemy's plans to try and draw us to respond to an external voice. God can take what the enemy intends for evil and turn it for good. He can cause the strategies of the enemy to be the very inspiration that inspires us to draw upon the strength of His Spirit within our hearts. It is Christ in us that is the hope of glory and Christ in us is the secret to hearing God in all things. God is not trying to prove we are weak. He is proving His strength within us. He doesn't just want us to hear Him; He wants us to be transformed because we hear Him.

These words of the enemy's temptation in James chapter one are written in fishing terms. The enemy doesn't know what is inside of our hearts, but he is fishing to draw upon our weaknesses. He puts a piece of carnality, a piece of meat, some bait, upon a hook and draws it past the nose of everyone. Some, who do not have the weakness for that particular bait upon the hook, do not even notice the temptation. Others, who have a weakness for that particular bait upon the hook, sniff as the bait passes by. The enemy, notices the attraction and begins to dangle the bait in front of us. Like fishing for a codfish, he begins to chum with the dance of temptation before our senses. It is not a sin

109

to be tempted, it is only when we bite the hook that life is given to the weakness that exists in our hearts. The power of belief, the power of the stronghold, is not in the bait of the enemy. It is in the weakness of our own hearts. God allows the temptation to come, because He knows that greater is the One inside of us. He wants the hearing of our souls to come by the hearing of our spirits – our spirits made alive by His Holy Spirit through the hearing of faith. He doesn't just want us to know how to pass the test. He wants to make us non-temptable by the transforming power of His voice in our hearts. Who we are and who we become is more important than what we do.

Fleshly lusts (our own way) war against our souls and hinder us from hearing God. God doesn't want to sweep our weaknesses under the rug. He doesn't want to hide them. He wants to heal them. A parent's job is not to teach their children to do good or merely avoid evil. It is to train them to hear God's voice. They are to train their children not to go their own way.

Galatians 5:19-21 Now the works of the flesh are evident, which are: adultery, fornication, uncleanness, lewdness, idolatry, sorcery, hatred, contentions, jealousies, outbursts of wrath, selfish ambitions, dissensions, heresies, envy, murders, drunkenness, revelries, and the like; of which I tell you beforehand, just as I also told you in time past, that those who practice such things will not inherit the kingdom of God.

The inheritance of the kingdom of God is not merely a matter of going to heaven when we die. Salvation by mercy will get us into heaven, but salvation by grace will empower us to bring heavenly realities into the world in which we live. Hearing God is about bringing His life into our worlds.

When it comes to hearing God, we must be aware of things that will hinder us from hearing Him. The voice of God is a voice to our hearts, not our heads. God speaks to our spirits and then our spirits flood our souls with thoughts, reasoning, emotions, and a will that is inspired by

God. When we keep our hearts right towards God and others we can trust the desires that come from within. If we become self-seeking, self-gratifying, self-sufficient, or self-defending in some way, we end up being damaged within with a bitter root in our hearts. When this happens, we hear God in our hearts but then we twist, manipulate, argue with, and hinder in some way what we think we hear Him saying in our heads. The good thing is, we are practitioners. Like doctors, we practice. We are seeking to practice our ability to hear God. If we practice we will get better in hearing Him.

Our heart is key to hearing God. It is important that we keep our hearts right before God so that His voice is not hindered in any way. We must never allow bitterness to infect our heart in a way that will cause His words to be twisted in our ears. Bitterness will lead us to buying into things that God never intended for us to walk in. A bitter heart will set us up for a deception and even a denial of the curses that are against us. Bitterness can tempt us to eat of the tree of the knowledge of good and evil and end up in a justice system of law and not of life.

Deuteronomy 29:16-19 "(for you know that we dwelt in the land of Egypt and that we came through the nations which you passed by, and you saw their abominations and their idols which were among them—wood and stone and silver and gold); so that there may not be among you man or woman or family or tribe, whose heart turns away today from the LORD our God, to go and serve the gods of these nations, and that there may not be among you a root bearing bitterness or wormwood; and so it may not happen, when he hears the words of this curse, that he blesses himself in his heart, saying, 'I shall have peace, even though I follow the dictates of my heart'— as though the drunkard could be included with the sober."

These verses are a testimony of living the way those in the world live. If we live with a self-seeking, self-gratifying attitude we will suffer the consequences of a government of self. People in the world aren't practicing intimacy with God and therefore the way of their hearts are not right before Him. As children of God, we cannot act the same.

Deuteronomy 29:20 "The LORD would not spare him; for then the anger of the LORD and His jealousy would burn against that man, and every curse that is written in this book would settle on him, and the LORD would blot out his name from under heaven."

God is not self-seeking in His ways. He doesn't need anything from anyone. His nature is to give life, to give breath, and to give all things to all people (Acts 17:25). When we don't allow Him to be the source of life in our hearts He is jealous on our behalf. Not jealous because we are not giving Him what He thinks He deserves. He is jealous because we are not allowing Him to give us what only He can give. We must understand His jealousy from the character of God, not the character of our own self-seeking flesh.

Deuteronomy 29:21-26 "And the LORD would separate him from all the tribes of Israel for adversity, according to all the curses of the covenant that are written in this Book of the Law, so that the coming generation of your children who rise up after you, and the foreigner who comes from a far land, would say, when they see the plagues of that land and the sicknesses which the LORD has laid on it: 'The whole land is brimstone, salt, and burning; it is not sown, nor does it bear, nor does any grass grow there, like the overthrow of Sodom and Gomorrah, Admah, and Zeboiim, which the LORD overthrew in His anger and His wrath.' All nations would say, 'Why has the LORD done so to this land? What does the heat of this great anger mean?' Then men would say: 'Because they have forsaken the covenant of the LORD God of their fathers, which He made with them when He brought them out of the land of Egypt; for they went and served other gods and worshipped them, gods that they did not know and that He had not given to them.'"

These verses are Old Covenant verses, but they are the shadow of a New Covenant reality in Christ. When we choose to live apart from a trust relationship with God in our hearts we choose a testimony of living a life where the consequence of violating laws reaps the fruit of death. God doesn't want anyone to live by laws but laws are a testimony of the boundaries of true life. God's wrath was never willingly against people, it is against the things that destroy life. When we hold on to things that destroy life we reap the consequence of destruction.

Deuteronomy 29:27-28 "Then the anger of the LORD was aroused against this land, to bring on it every curse that is written in this book. And the LORD uprooted them from their land in anger, in wrath, and in great indignation, and cast them into another land, as it is this day.'"

God does not curse people; people curse themselves when they choose to cling to the things that are cursed. God wants all people to know an intimate relationship with Him that leads to life. If we love something more than Him, the thing we love will become the very thing that we become uprooted from. God wants people to see that the things that humans allow to replace Him in their lives are a curse, and only life in Him brings true blessings. If we willingly jump off a tall building we cannot blame God for a judgment of the law of gravity. Gravity was intended to keep us on the ground and if we violate its purpose we reap the consequence of our own actions.

Deuteronomy 29:29 "The secret things belong to the LORD our God, but those things which are revealed belong to us and to our children forever, that we may do all the words of this law."

When we harbor bitterness in our hearts, we often allow other voices to become a life source to our souls. When we fail to see God meeting our need in an area and we reach out to something else to meet that need – that is bitterness. Shame, jealousy, and condemnation can all be evidences of bitterness in our hearts. God wants to reveal His secret things to us, but if we fail to let God heal the bitter places in our hearts, the secret things won't belong to us and to our children. Harboring bitterness in our hearts can result in generational hindrances and consequences.

Chapter 8

Attitudes and Hearing

Hearing God begins with an attitude of wanting to hear Him. The source of attitude is desire. When we are hungry for food, we desire to eat. If we truly hunger for God we will find Him. When we hunger to hear Him we hear Him. The point of hearing Him is life. His words give us life. A relationship with Him makes us come alive. People who don't want to know God don't hear Him because they don't want to hear Him. The wicked don't hear God because they don't desire Him in their hearts.

Job 21:14-15 "Yet they say to God, 'Depart from us, for we do not desire the knowledge of Your ways. Who is the Almighty, that we should serve Him? And what profit do we have if we pray to Him?'"

The attitude of those who do not desire to hear God is an attitude of self-seeking. They don't want to hear Him because they are afraid of losing what they want if they hear Him. They desire their own way more than they desire the way of God.

Hearing God has its foundation rooted in an attitude to hear Him. We must open up our hearts to hear Him. God doesn't want us to approach Him with an attitude of doing something to gain His favor. He wants us to come with open ears to hear Him and His desires. When we know how much He loves us, we open our hearts to hear Him. When we love Him we desire to hear Him.

Psalms 40:6-8 Sacrifice and offering You did not desire; My ears You have opened. Burnt offering and sin offering You did not require. Then I said, "Behold, I come; in the scroll of the Book it is written of me. I delight to do Your will, O my God, And Your law is within my heart."

To hear God we have to have a desire to hear God. This involves a desire to see His will, not ours, done in our lives. God doesn't want our sacrifices and our offerings. He wants a personal relationship with us. We don't hear God so we can make the right sacrifices or give the right offerings. We hear God because we want to know Him. When we want to know Him we realize that He wants us and we receive a revelation of a two-way partnership where hearing Him becomes a matter of love and relationship.

Sometimes we hear Him clearly, but then our own desires interfere with our understanding of what He says. There is a difference between revelation, interpretation, and application of what God says to us. We may hear the words He speaks to us, but we may not understand what they mean or how His words will play out in our lives. When Jesus asked His disciples who He was, Peter heard the voice of God in his heart. He understood that Jesus was the Christ, the Son of the living God. This was a revelation from God to his heart. Jesus commended him on his hearing the voice of God and even gave keys to Peter's destiny in hearing. Peter had a revelation that was right and true.

Matthew 16:13-19 When Jesus came into the region of Caesarea Philippi, He asked His disciples, saying, "Who do men say that I, the Son of Man, am?" So they said, "Some say John the Baptist, some Elijah, and others Jeremiah or one of the prophets." 15 He said to them, "But who do you say that I am?" And Simon Peter answered and said, "You are the Christ, the Son of the living God." Jesus answered and said to him, "Blessed are you, Simon Bar-Jonah, for flesh and blood has not revealed this to you, but My Father who is in heaven. And I also say to you that you are Peter, and on this rock I will build My church, and the gates of Hades shall not prevail against it. And I will give you the keys of the kingdom of heaven, and whatever you bind on earth will be bound in heaven, and whatever you loose on earth will be loosed in heaven."

Although Peter had a pure revelation in hearing who Jesus really was, he also had preconceived ideas of what that meant. His desire for the Kingdom of God to be a testimony of the nation of Israel caused him to be blinded in his own heart towards the full revelation of what Jesus being the Christ, the Messiah, meant. When Jesus began to speak of His imminent suffering in Jerusalem, Peter rebuked him. His understanding was that Jesus would set up the kingdom as the head of the nation of Israel and His kingdom would be manifested as an external kingdom of triumph over the enemies of Israel.

Matthew 16:21-23 From that time Jesus began to show to His disciples that He must go to Jerusalem, and suffer many things from the elders and chief priests and scribes, and be killed, and be raised again the third day. Then Peter took Him aside and began to rebuke Him, saying, "Far be it from You, Lord; this shall not happen to You!" But He turned and said to Peter, "Get behind Me, Satan! You are an offense to Me, for you are not mindful of the things of God, but the things of men."

Peter was not mindful of the things of God, because He had preconceived ideas as to what those things were. Peter's mindset caused him a few rough moments in the days that followed, but Jesus prayed for him and God's grace was enough to turn things for good in Peter's life. A key to hearing God clearly is found in our willingness to lay aside our personal desires for the desires of God. Taking up our cross is not making the sacrifice that Jesus made for us on the cross of Calvary, it is in our willingness to set aside our personal desires for God and the wellbeing of others. When we embrace an attitude of His will being done we position our souls to hear Him from our hearts.

Matthew 16:24-25 Then Jesus said to His disciples, "If anyone desires to come after Me, let him deny himself, and take up his cross, and follow Me. For whoever desires to save his life will lose it, but whoever loses his life for My sake will find it."

Chapter 9

Learning To Do His Will

Learning to hear God means learning to do His will. If we are not willing in our hearts to do what He wants or become what He desires for us to become, we are really saying we do not want to hear Him. When we hear God change happens in our hearts. If we are not willing to change we are not willing to hear Him. He is not going to become like us so we can hear Him. He will become as us, but He will not become like us. Because He comes as us, He expects us to become as He is. When we see Him we become like Him because we see Him as He is.

He became flesh and moved into the neighborhood of humanity; but He didn't change the character, nature, way, power, or authority of whom He was in the process. He was the Word of God made flesh so that all flesh could be given the power to become a testimony of who He is. Anyone can become an expression of the likeness and the image of their heavenly Father through the grace given by Jesus Christ. He empathizes with us in our weaknesses, but He didn't succumb to our weaknesses. He made a way for us to boldly come before Him to receive mercy for our failures and find grace for change in our lives (Heb. 4:16). This is a testimony of hearing God.

God's ways are not our ways. When we hear Him in our hearts His ways begin to become the nature of our way in life. His Spirit in us is a testimony of His power that changes everything from within. This means we must be willing to embrace what we don't think we will like in order to receive a revelation in our heart as to how wonderful His change within us can be. Our natural man will not immediately desire it, so we must stir up our inner man to override our natural desires. When we hear Him we are changed.

Luke 5:39 "And no one, having drunk old wine, immediately desires new; for he says, 'The old is better.'"

In order to have a lifestyle of hearing God, we must delight ourselves in God. This is more than simply desiring to hear Him. It is a matter of committing our way to Him and trusting Him. It involves not trusting in our own understanding. It is a matter of acknowledging Him in all of our ways. If we desire Him we will also desire to hear what He says to us. The evidence of our hearing Him is change within us.

Psalms 37:4 Delight yourself also in the LORD, And He shall give you the desires of your heart.

The key in this verse is the Lord, not the hearing. When we delight ourselves in the Lord He puts new desires in our hearts. Our 'want to' changes – this is the fruit of hearing Him. This is not a testimony of legalistically doing what He said to others long ago. It is not a matter of legalistically attempting to do what is written in His word. It is a matter of hearing Him speak to our hearts. What He says will be confirmed through the principles, patterns, and values found in the words that are expressions of His voice in the past. The Bible will be a witness to the voice we are hearing, but the hearing will be a hearing of faith. It is a hearing that comes from inside our hearts when we embrace His presence. It is a hearing that comes from inside our hearts when we embrace His Lordship. He is the one who determines the boundaries and the flow of life-giving water within those boundaries. The fruit of hearing Him is seen in the desire of our hearts. It is manifested through the works that come out from the desires within us. That fruit will be motivated by faith; it will inspire hope in others, and will express God's love in the world. We need God's rhema word resident within us. This is His personally spoken word in our hearts.

John 15:7 "If you abide in Me, and My words abide in you, you will ask what you desire, and it shall be done for you."

The 'words' that abide in us are not a memorization of His written word. They are 'rhema' expressions of God in our hearts. They are the now voice of God inside of us. When we abide in Him, hearing Him comes naturally.

We must learn to crucify the flesh so that we can learn to hear God's voice. We do not crucify the flesh by attacking our flesh or setting our minds to bind it. We crucify the flesh by indulging in the presence of God in our lives. When we embrace Him we embrace the passions and desires of life, and we receive the life that comes by His Spirit. That life is more powerful than the carnal desires of our flesh.

Galatians 5:24 ...and those who are Christ's have crucified the flesh with its passions and desires.

Ephesians 2:13 But now in Christ Jesus you who once were far off have been made near by the blood of Christ.

When we choose to live our lives near to Him we hear Him. He made a way for us to come near to Him and to live with Him. The key to crucifying our old desires is to simply live our lives near to Him where we hear Him. When we hear Him, we are changed. If we choose to move away from Him, we choose to hear something other than Him. Seeking knowing what to do in life is not the same as seeking knowing Him. When we seek what He can do, more than who He is, we can become twisted in our desires.

2 Timothy 4:3-4 For the time will come when they will not endure sound doctrine, but according to their own desires, because they have itching ears, they will heap up for themselves teachers; and they will turn their ears away from the truth, and be turned aside to fables.

We must be drawn to Him to hear Him. When we are drawn away from Him we become subject to the desires that are not His. Our hearing will be distorted and our testimony will be less than what He desires. We will hear what we want to hear and think it is Him speaking, but it is simply the twisting of His words in our minds to justify the desires of our own hearts.

James 1:14 But each one is tempted when he is drawn away by his own desires and enticed.

God wants us to receive His desires in our hearts. Our willingness to receive His desires is directly connected to our ability to hear Him clearly. Jesus is our example. He trusted His relationship with His Father more than the things He could feel or see. He was willing to change; therefore, He was always able to hear.

Matthew 26:36-41 Then Jesus came with them to a place called Gethsemane, and said to the disciples, "Sit here while I go and pray over there." And He took with Him Peter and the two sons of Zebedee, and He began to be sorrowful and deeply distressed. Then He said to them, "My soul is exceedingly sorrowful, even to death. Stay here and watch with Me." He went a little farther and fell on His face, and prayed, saying, "O My Father, if it is possible, let this cup pass from Me; nevertheless, not as I will, but as You will." Then He came to the disciples and found them asleep, and said to Peter, "What, could you not watch with Me one hour? Watch and pray, lest you enter into temptation. The spirit indeed is willing, but the flesh is weak."

The emphasis in these verses is not how weak the flesh is. It is in how willing the Spirit is. The Spirit is willing so we must commit our spirit to His Spirit to see His desires empower the actions of our lives. We must be awake in our hearts to Him and expect to hear Him. When we indulge in Him, we become like Him. It is not a matter of trying to destroy the flesh, but a matter of feeding the spirit. When we are willing to change, we hear what He says.

Chapter 10

Knowing the Will of God

1. Knowing the General Will to Know His Specific Will:

How can we know the will of God? When we think of the will of God in our lives we often think of the specific will of God. What is He saying to us? What does He want us to do? Who does He say we are? What should we do in a specific situation? The key to knowing the specific will of God in our lives is discovered when we excel in knowing the general will of God for all human lives. It is actually easy to know the general will of God when we seek to know who God is as a person. The general will of God is found in His word, since His word is a witness to who He is. The general will of God is for all to know Him, but if we don't know the general will we will be deceived into believing He only wants to know some. The general will of God reveals that mercy has triumphed over judgment but, if we don't know that general will, we will become propagators of judgment and susceptible to voices of condemnation. When we don't know the general will of God we become confused in understanding the specific will of God in our lives. When we don't know the general will of God we ask God illegitimate questions. We shouldn't ask God to do what He has already done. We need to position ourselves to fulfill the specifics of His general will. Because of the general will, I will prophesy. I can now discern the specific will of God in prophecy.

Let's look at an example of the general will of God for mankind. We can find a testimony of the general will in regard to God's plan for humanity in the book of Joel.

Joel 2:28-29 "And it shall come to pass afterward that I will pour out My Spirit on all flesh; your sons and your daughters shall prophesy, your old men shall dream dreams, your young men shall see visions. And also on My menservants and on My maidservants I will pour out My Spirit in those days."

These words were revealed as a New Covenant testimony in the second chapter of the book of Acts when God poured out His Holy Spirit upon the first expression of the body of Christ. One hundred twenty people in the upper room received a specific demonstration of the Holy Spirit's submersion, but the testimony was in agreement with the general will of God prophesied through the prophet Joel hundreds of years before the testimony of Pentecost in the book of Acts. The general will of God was that after the kingdom of a nation would come the testimony of the kingdom of God for all nations. After the last days of the kingdom of Israel, God would pour out His Spirit upon all flesh. The firstfruit of this New Covenant testimony of life was the fulfillment of Old Covenant Pentecost. This brought about a demonstration of the power of the Holy Spirit that would progress to all the tongues, tribes, peoples, and nations of the world. The general will of God pouring out His Spirit on all flesh set precedence for a specific fulfillment for some flesh. It was a prophetic Spirit that would change the destiny of all nations forever. I believe that the specific will of God is for each and everyone of us to experience the presence of the Holy Spirit in our lives in a unique and powerful way, but if we don't know the general will of God concerning His Holy Spirit upon all flesh we will not be able to believe for the specific will of God concerning the Holy Spirit upon our lives.

Another example can be found in the Scripture concerning the reconciliation of mankind. The general will of God reveals that God has reconciled all people to Himself and that we are ambassadors of reconciliation to the world. This is the general will of God, but there is also a specific will concerning how that looks in each of our lives.

2 Corinthians 5:18-21 Now all things are of God, who has reconciled us to Himself through Jesus Christ, and has given us the ministry of reconciliation, that is, that God was in Christ reconciling the world to Himself, not imputing their trespasses to them, and has committed to us the word of reconciliation. Now then, we are ambassadors for Christ, as though God were pleading through us: we implore you on Christ's behalf, be reconciled to God. For He made Him who knew no sin to be sin for us, that we might become the righteousness of God in Him.

When we are true in being ourselves we can reach the specific people that God has called each of us to reach. When I know that the general will of God says that I am an ambassador of reconciliation, I can then seek to hear God in the specifics of how that may look in my life.

The general will of God says that when two people agree concerning what they ask it will be done for them on earth. This is a general will, but the specific will of how that looks and what that agreement should be upon can only be discovered when we know that the general will is to agree. The specific will then comes through specific points of instruction in life.

Matthew 18:19 "Again I say to you that if two of you agree on earth concerning anything that they ask, it will be done for them by My Father in heaven."

There are many examples we can use concerning the general will of God and it is only when we know the general will of God that we can be directed in the specific will of God. The general will of God could apply to things like:
- The keeping of covenants
- Willingness to work
- Honoring God with our finances
- Living with sexual purity
- Keeping connected to relationships in the body of Christ
- Personal integrity

- God's willingness to heal
- The forgiveness of sins
- And countless other examples in found in the Scriptures

When we know the general will of God, how does God make His specific will known to us? God reveals His specific will through dreams, like the dreams of Joseph. I have had many times where God has revealed His specific will to me through a dream or a vision in the spirit. God can speak through an audible voice, like he did with Moses. As I have surveyed various groups of believers in ministry training, I have discovered that 15% to 20% of those I survey have heard the audible voice of God. This is not a better way of hearing God – it is just one way. It is one of many in hearing the specific will of God in our lives. Just as significant is the still small voice in our hearts, as it was in the days of Elijah and his experience with God when coming out of the cave. An angel of the Lord is another way of God revealing His specific voice. I know of many testimonies where people have come to Christ or heard His voice through an angel of the Lord, like the testimony of Gideon. We have an example in the New Testament of the angel Gabriel speaking to Mary at the conception of Jesus. Saul of Tarsus experienced a personal appearance of Jesus that transformed him to become Paul the apostle. I have heard stories of many people in Muslim countries having a personal appearance of Jesus in their conversion to Christianity. I have spoken with many people in the Apache nation that have experienced the same. There are many different levels and experiences in the realm of angels. I have three angels that work with me on a regular basis in ministry. They are not greater than I am, but only serve as ministers with me in seeing the will of God made known in people's lives. The Holy Spirit is the senior partner in our relationship, I am a son of God, and angels are ministering spirits sent to help. Personal prophecy is a means of hearing God specifically. This can come in dynamic or subtler ways. Divine revelation knowledge that comes by reading God's word can be a way of specifically hearing God. Once we know the general will of God in His word, the specific will of God will often flood our souls in various subjects. When we receive a revelation of healing, we hear God in His word concerning healing. I have had this happen many times in my life concerning the kingdom of God, the baptism of the Holy Spirit, an understanding of grace, New Covenant realities, and many other areas of revelation. Divine revelation or personal instruction to our hearts can come through the preaching or teaching of God's word through sent authority in our lives. God will even speak through people that don't know God, or even secular societies around us. I often refer to them as 'secular prophets.' They are hungry to hear something so they hear God, but they don't know it is Him. They will twist what He says to their own agendas, but at least they are hearing something. In the church we are often busy trying to preserve what God said yesterday and we miss the fresh things He is saying now. I pay attention to the 'secular prophets' around me; not to believe what they are saying, but to turn to God to hear what He is really saying. God can speak through things. He spoke through a donkey to Baalam. The Bible is full of prophetic symbolisms and God still uses prophetic symbolisms in things around us to get our attention in what He wants to say to us. None of these things override the general will of God. We must know the general will of God in order to properly discern the specific will of God in our lives. Intimacy with God in His character is the foundation to hearing God in His power.

We must study God's general will or we will be susceptible to deception in the specific ways of hearing God. The apostle Paul instructed the church not to believe an angel that brought them something different than the good news that He had delivered to the church (Gal. 1:8) and that even the devil seeks to disguise himself as an angel of light (2 Cor. 11:14). The specific will of God doesn't simply come from a supernatural experience, an encounter with an angel, or some sign and wonder. The specific will of God comes by many diverse ways, but it is only properly discerned when we know the general will of God that is true to the character of God. Any voice revealing God's specific will in our lives must be witnessed by the character, nature, way, power, and authority of who God was, is, and always will be.

Deuteronomy 13:1-4 "If there arises among you a prophet or a dreamer of dreams, and he gives you a sign or a wonder, and the sign or the wonder comes to pass, of which he spoke to you, saying, 'Let us go after other gods' — which you have not known —'and let us serve them,' you shall not listen to the words of that prophet or that dreamer of dreams, for the Lord your God is testing you to know whether you love the Lord your God with all your heart and with all your soul. You shall walk after the Lord your God and fear Him, and keep His commandments and obey His voice; you shall serve Him and hold fast to Him."

The enemy doesn't tell you he is your enemy. He disguises his voice to sound like God. Another god could be ministry, work, human relationships, false doctrine, or anything that exalts itself above intimacy with God in your life.

2. Receiving God's Specific Will

Those who desire to hear God hear Him. He is speaking to all people, but not all people are listening. When we desire to hear Him we hear what He is saying, and we even inspire Him to speak specifically to us in many ways. He even fills our hearts with desires that are expressions of His thoughts within us. It seems like it is us, but it only comes when we delight ourselves in Him. When we decide to trust Him, commit our ways to Him, and acknowledge Him in all things we begin to hear Him in all things.

We must delight ourselves in the Lord more than a dream, an angel, an audible voice, divine revelation, a prophetic word, or any thing. God's voice is not a supernatural experience. His voice invokes supernatural things, but those supernatural things are merely the evidence of His presence. He doesn't just want to give us supernatural liberty, He wants to give us life-giving boundaries through His supernatural ability. The Spirit of the Lord is a boundary that gives definition to the ability to hear Him specifically. It is not merely a spirit of liberty. It is the Spirit of the Lord, and He gives true liberty. This is not merely doing what we want, but being filled in our hearts and minds with all that He wants.

There is clear evidence to His voice in our hearts. The fruit of the Spirit accompanies the voice of God. It is the evidence of His word, will, and way in our lives. If the fruit of the Spirit is not there, then the voice is something other than the voice of God.

Galatians 5:22-23 But the fruit of the Spirit is love, joy, peace, longsuffering, kindness, goodness, faithfulness, gentleness, self-control. Against such there is no law.

The fruit of the Spirit is sometimes easy when we see it as love, joy, and peace, but what about the fruit of longsuffering, faithfulness, or self-control? If a word is from God it will be filled with the fruit of God in its substance.

If you hear a word that invokes you to think something must happen or you will die, it is not likely a word from God. Words like that often translate to be something like this: "I'm going to die if they don't notice me," or "I'm going to die if I am not important." Word's from God reveal that we already are valuable; they don't make us valuable. Word's from God inspire us to even bless our enemies. They do not provoke us to get even with our enemies. Words from God produce life and they are a testimony of the character of the fruit of Holy Spirit. To know God's voice and will in our lives is to be spiritually-minded. Being spiritually-minded is being filled with the testimony of the fruit of the Spirit.

Romans 8:6 For to be carnally minded is death, but to be spiritually minded is life and peace.

Life and peace are a testimony of right thinking in Christ. Peace is a testimony of there being no gap between God and us. We have full access to His presence. Life is a testimony of the power of God's grace at work in our lives. It is the evidence that God is in us. God's peace and life are progressive in our lives. God blesses some things that after a while He doesn't. When a baby has their first birthday they usually put cake all over themselves and we call it cute. When they get

127

to be a teenager we expect them to keep the food off of their bodies. When a child begins to walk they are mostly falling forward and falling down a lot, but we joyfully call it walking. When they get to be older we expect them to learn the skills of balance and accuracy. Just as we grow as natural people, God also allows us to grow spiritually. What is blessed in one season is only meant to lead to greater maturity in the seasons that follow. Even when it comes to expressions of the Spirit we must not allow our carnal attitudes to affect our spiritual actions. A fruit of praying in tongues cannot be 'frustration'. If you are frustrated while praying in tongues there is something wrong in our expression. Warring against the devil must be a testimony of turning on the light, not trying to put out the darkness. The ultimate testimony of the voice of God in our hearts is peace.

Philippians 4:4-7 Rejoice in the Lord always. Again I will say, rejoice! Let your gentleness be known to all men. The Lord is at hand. Be anxious for nothing, but in everything by prayer and supplication, with thanksgiving, let your requests be made known to God; and the peace of God, which surpasses all understanding, will guard your hearts and minds through Christ Jesus.

Doubt and fear are not the evidence. Peace is! The testimony of Jesus in our lives is peace. The Holy Spirit is God with us and He brings the peace of God in all things. A prerequisite to finding the peace of God is to choose to rejoice in the Lord in all things and in every situation. A gentle attitude towards others prepares our hearts to hear God. We cannot allow anxiousness for solutions, deliverances, healings, provisions, or anything to rob us from an abiding relationship with God that allows us to know His voice within. His voice is confirmed with a peace that surpasses all of our understanding.

When God speaks it inspires faith in our hearts. His voice does not invoke fear. Faith comes from hearing God in our hearts. His voice within is the confirmation of presence in our hearts. He has made peace for us. It was not something we did, but an act of God's love when His mercy triumphed over the judgment that was against us in our lives. Sin separated us from God, but God gave a power through the gift of His Son to destroy the sin. We cannot willingly continue to sin and expect to reap the benefits of God's peace in our lives; but the way to return to God is not by works we have done, it is by believing His love. There doesn't need to be a gap between us and God in our hearts. We cannot do the things that are not true to His character and expect to sustain His peace, but His peace will give us access to His grace that will change our character to become like Him. The Holy Spirit in us brings the peace of God in all things. As I have stated, "a prerequisite to finding the peace of God is to choose to rejoice in the Lord in all things and in every situation. A gentle attitude towards others prepares our hearts to hear God. We cannot allow anxiousness for solutions, deliverances, healings, provisions, or anything to rob us from an abiding relationship with God that allows us to know His voice within. His voice is confirmed with a peace that surpasses all of our understanding."

Jesus promised the gift of peace in our hearts through the gift of the Helper, the Holy Spirit.

John 14:22-31 Judas (not Iscariot) said to Him, "Lord, how is it that You will manifest Yourself to us, and not to the world?" Jesus answered and said to him, "If anyone loves Me, he will keep My word; and My Father will love him, and We will come to him and make Our home with him. He who does not love Me does not keep My words; and the word which you hear is not Mine but the Father's who sent Me. These things I have spoken to you while being present with you. But the Helper, the Holy Spirit, whom the Father will send in My name, He will teach you all things, and bring to your remembrance all things that I said to you. Peace I leave with you, My peace I give to you; not as the world gives do I give to you. Let not your heart be troubled, neither let it be afraid. You have heard Me say to you, 'I am going away and coming back to you.' If you loved Me, you would rejoice because I said, 'I am going to the Father,' for My Father is greater than I. And now I have told you before it comes, that when it does come to pass, you may believe. I will no longer talk much with you, for the ruler of this world is coming, and he has nothing in Me. But that the world may know that I love the Father, and as the Father gave Me commandment, so I do. Arise, let us go from here."

It was the peace of God that was given to us. It was the peace of God that confirms that we are not separate from God; we can depend upon Him in all things. When events of trouble in the world happen it is time for the church to rise up with peace, not fear. We must release His Spirit in our hearts. We have peace with and from God that empowers us to hear Him and to trust what He says more than what we can see with our eyes, hear with our natural ears, or expect in our natural understanding. Hearing God is established upon a foundation of being one with Him.

1 John 3:19-24 And by this we know that we are of the truth, and shall assure our hearts before Him. For if our heart condemns us, God is greater than our heart, and knows all things. Beloved, if our heart does not condemn us, we have confidence toward God. And whatever we ask we receive from Him, because we keep His commandments and do those things that are pleasing in His sight. And this is His commandment: that we should believe on the name of His Son Jesus Christ and love one another, as He gave us commandment. Now he who keeps His commandments abides in Him, and He in him. And by this we know that He abides in us, by the Spirit whom He has given us.

When we are one with God in our hearts, we know it. We can tell when our own hearts condemn us. It is not God who condemns us, but our own hearts can condemn us when we choose to live our lives separate from God's will and way. We must live our lives as children of God to know the peace that is truly available to all people. When we have the peace of God in our hearts we live our lives to bring the life of God to others. We don't do this to be justified before God. We do it because we know we are justified. When we know the power of His love we choose to live our lives in a way that reveals His love to others. To live for ourselves is to live one with ourselves, not one with God.

To live for God and the wellbeing of others is a testimony of being one with God. It is a testimony of His peace.

The will of God in your life will bring life to others. It is broader than you expect. It results from who you are, not what you do. Hearing God is not about knowing what to do. It is about knowing who God is and then in turn discovering who you are in Him. When you know who you are, you will know what to do. I don't believe that the will of God is to do one thing in life, but perhaps thousands of things that are all true to who you are. Who you are, is the one thing; and what you do can be many things. Hearing God is about becoming and being, not working and doing.

I have discovered that God speaks to me in regard to my individual purpose and grace, and in terms of chapters or seasons in my life. My prophetic purpose and grace is to expose false walls and to activate the pursuit of truth. This doesn't mean that I look for false walls to expose. It simply means that I naturally expose them without trying to think about it. I also naturally inspire others to pursue truth. That is to pursue something beyond what they have known before. For this reason, I am better off organizing a warehouse, than simply inventorying one. I also have an apostolic purpose and grace to bring New Covenant life and grace to barren places in the earth. I don't look for barren places; I simply bring New Covenant life and grace to them when I encounter them. For this reason I am better at pioneering new things than I am at simply settling for old ones. In regard to seasons, I was a senior pastor for twenty years and God spoke to me in the context of direction in the local church. Today I bring equipping and resources to the body of Christ. God doesn't speak to me in direction for the local church, but rather speaks to me toward becoming an equipper and resource to many churches. If I hear direction for the local church I need to submit it to those responsible. It is not my responsibility and I will not hear clearly if I assume the responsibility of giving direction. The season has changed and therefore my responsibility has changed.

How can you know the specific will of God in your life? The

specific will of God will always fall within the boundaries of your responsibility. If you are not responsible, God will not speak to you in regard to an area. If you hear a voice that seems to be God concerning an area in which you are not responsible you are simply being tested to know who you really are. If you hear something for a responsibility you don't carry do you ask to hear more? This would be irresponsible on your part. It is none of your business. I have found this true on many occasions in my life. To some I am a prophet, but to others I am not. I cannot simply go to any house group in the city and speak prophetic words of direction and think that I am in the will of God. I can only give directional words in places I am responsible to and for. To go beyond that measure is simply being irresponsible and blaming it on God.

Responsibilities can change. King David's journey started out as a shepherd boy, progressed to being a cheese-deliverer, a giant-killer, a servant of Saul, a worship leader, an appeaser-of-demons, a javelin-dodger, a humble servant in refuge, and finally the King of Israel. He had the anointing of a king in the entire journey, but only the authority for each season he was in. Hearing the specific will of God in our lives is directly related to who we are and to what we are responsible for in any given season in our lives.

Chapter 11

What Is God's Will?

1. A Will of the Spirit

Hearing God is not a matter of having some supernatural experience that is out of this world. It is a supernatural experience in this world, but it doesn't have to be mystical or weird. It is the life of God's Spirit in our spirits that flood our souls and empower our actions in life to be led by God's voice. God is Spirit so we must unite our spirits to His Spirit in our hearts. When hearing God's voice, and knowing God's will, we must also unite our souls with our spirits in the place where God speaks.

Hebrews 4:12 For the word of God is living and powerful, and sharper than any two-edged sword, piercing even to the division of soul and spirit, and of joints and marrow, and is a discerner of the thoughts and intents of the heart.

As I presented before, the word of God in this Scripture is the logos of God. It is something that has been expressed by God. This would include the Scriptures, but it is not limited to them. It is any thing that God has expressed. When we come face-to-face with something that God has expressed it activates the voice of God in our hearts. It causes our spirits, souls, and bodies to become united in the will of God.

When we expose ourselves to the word of God, it draws the Holy Spirit within us to flood our spirits, in turn our spirits flood our souls, and our souls empower the actions of our lives. This can happen when we read the Scriptures, because the Scriptures include the expression of God in the past. It can happen when we soak in worship, because worship is an expression of the manifested word of God and it can draw the Holy Spirit within our spirits and empower our spirits to flood our souls. It unites our spirits and our souls. We are not a body with a soul and a spirit. We are spirit, soul, and body. We are spiritual – spirit-natural. Our minds must be flooded with God's will. Our emotions must become His emotions. Our souls can't just be an expression of our own minds, wills, reasoning, and emotions. Our souls must become living souls by our spirits made alive within us. It is then that God's mind, will, reasoning, and emotions become our will from within. We do this by constantly submitting to, and submerging ourselves in, the expressions of God. The word of God pierces through our souls to our spirits, the joint to the marrow in the bone, and the thought to the discerner of the thought within. When this happens what is within us becomes the source of knowing the will of God. God is Spirit and His voice is a voice to our spirits. It is then that our spirits become the voice within us that empowers our souls.

1 Corinthians 2:10-13 But God has revealed them to us through His Spirit. For the Spirit searches all things, yes, the deep things of God. For what man knows the things of a man except the spirit of the man which is in him? Even so no one knows the things of God except the Spirit of God. Now we have received, not the spirit of the world, but the Spirit who is from God, that we might know the things that have been freely given to us by God. These things we also speak, not in words which man's wisdom teaches but which the Holy Spirit teaches, comparing spiritual things with spiritual.

The mysteries of God are made known to our spirits. It is then that our souls begin to become transformed to His understanding. It is only in our spirits that we can know what has been freely given to us by God. God teaches our spirits, not our heads. He empowers our hearts. Christ in us is the hope of glory, not Christ to us. In order to know and understand the will of God in our lives we must unite our spirits with the Spirit of God. We must submit our minds to the mind of Christ within us, which is a mind of the Spirit.

2 Timothy 1:6-7 Therefore I remind you to stir up the gift of God which is in you through the laying on of my hands. For God has not given us a spirit of fear, but of power and of love and of a sound mind.

Paul told Timothy to stir up the gift that was within him. I believe that gift is the Holy Spirit and it is by Christ's Spirit within us that we can know God's power, love, and understanding. We can do practical things to activate the Spirit of God in our own spirits within. Praying in tongues will stir up what is within us. We can sing songs of praise and worship to stir up what is in us. Deciding to come together with other believers can stir up what is within us. Being around other believers, exposes us to what God has written in their hearts and minds. This inspires the letter of the Holy Spirit in our own hearts and minds. Taking a walk in nature and considering God and His ways can stir up what is within us. Moving from the back of the room in church to the front of the room can stir up what is within us. Going forward in worship can stir up what is within us. Researching a word, topic, or subject that comes to our hearts can stir up what is within us. This can involve reading the Scriptures, as well as doing research on the natural way those words, topics, and subjects can be seen in the world or how they have been seen by others.

God is Spirit and His will is a spiritual will. We are spirit and natural in our make-up and this is what makes us spiritual people. We are pilgrims in our journey of life. We were born in heaven, but we live in the earth. We are resident aliens in the world. Our citizenship is in heaven, but a work visa has been given to us for this world. To do this, we must know that hearing God is something that is within us and that our path in this world is empowered by the Spirit of God in our hearts.

Ephesians 3:14-21 For this reason I bow my knees to the Father of our Lord Jesus Christ, from whom the whole family in heaven and earth is named, that He would grant you, according to the riches of His glory, to be strengthened with might through His Spirit in the inner man, that Christ may dwell in your hearts through faith; that you, being rooted and grounded in love, may be able to comprehend with all the saints what is the width and length and depth and height– to know the love of Christ which passes knowledge; that you may be filled with all the fullness of God. Now to Him who is able to do exceedingly abundantly above all that we ask or think, according to the power that works in us, to Him be glory in the church by Christ Jesus throughout all ages, world without end. Amen.

There is something within us that surpasses our own understanding. It is the presence of Christ in our hearts. This is the key to hearing God's voice, knowing His will, and being empowered to walk in it in this life. In this process, some individuals are a sign and wonder, but this isn't normal life. Hearing God can include strange, unexplainable experiences – but it doesn't always look like that. God is usually very practical and real. God's voice is very relational.

God wants to speak to us as a Father to His children. This is why He has made a way for His Spirit to live within us. Jesus made a way for our spirits to abide in the Spirit of God and for God's Spirit to abide in the spirit of man. It is in the spirit realm of man where divine love and faith operate. How do we get the realm of the spirit to operate in the realm of the visible? It starts with each of us yielding to truth, and then stirring up the Spirit of Truth within us. The Spirit of Truth is the life of the Holy Spirit within our hearts. We find God in what He has expressed in this world, so we can hear His personal expressions in our hearts. The expressions of God in the past are in creation, the Scriptures, and the testimonies of others. It is through exposing ourselves to these expressions that we draw God's Spirit to our spirit and this sparks a unity of our spirit, soul, and body for the will of God in our lives.

The evidence of an activated spirit is a living soul. The soul is the area of our emotions, reasoning, imaginations and desires. Emotions aren't bad, reasoning isn't bad, imaginations aren't bad, neither are human desires. It is their source that makes them good or bad. We must learn how to connect our spirit to God's Spirit to receive what God knows, thinks, feels, and desires. We must learn how to draw the testimony of heaven into our hearts and then how to allow those heavenly realities to flood the depths of our souls.

To do this, we must unite our souls with our spirits once our spirits have united with God's Spirit. When we do this our emotions, reasoning, imaginations, and desires become as God's are. Our desires (self-desires) will then become God-desires.

Psalms 25:1-5 To You, O LORD, I lift up my soul. O my God, I trust in You; Let me not be ashamed; Let not my enemies triumph over me. Indeed, let no one who waits on You be ashamed; let those be ashamed who deal treacherously without cause. Show me Your ways, O LORD; Teach me Your paths. Lead me in Your truth and teach me, for You are the God of my salvation; on You I wait all the day.

What does it mean to wait upon God? Waiting upon God is not waiting for God to do something. It is choosing to abide in His presence. It is choosing to draw near to Him and to intertwine our hearts with all that He is. This is practically activated by allowing the Spirit of revelation to rise in our hearts as we choose to willingly draw near to God.

Isaiah 40:31 But those who wait on the LORD shall renew their strength; they shall mount up with wings like eagles, they shall run and not be weary, they shall walk and not faint.

Waiting on the Lord doesn't just mean waiting for Him to do something. It is to join yourself to the hope of His presence. It involves taking hold of Him and then choosing to not let Him go. It is the place of His abiding presence that the hope of His glory is found. Christ in you is the New Covenant reality of waiting upon the Lord. This is the source of your strength and you must choose to attach to Christ within you in a consistent and constant manner.

Psalms 119:14-18 I have rejoiced in the way of Your testimonies, as much as in all riches. I will meditate on Your precepts, and contemplate Your ways. I will delight myself in Your statutes; I will not forget Your word. Deal bountifully with Your servant, that I may live and keep Your word. Open my eyes, that I may see wondrous things from Your law.

One way of stirring the Spirit of God within us is to expose ourselves to His expressions in the past. The Scriptures reveal the character, nature, way, power, and authority of God. We don't go to the Scriptures to find out what is wrong with us. We go to the Scriptures to learn what God is like as a person. The more we know who He is, the clearer we will recognize His voice within our hearts. We must choose to know that He loves us and that He wants a relationship with each of us. We must not see ourselves as enemies of God, but as friends. This is foundational to joining our spirits to His in our hearts. We can trust Him, therefore, we also know that we can hear Him.

Proverbs 3:5-6 Trust in the LORD with all your heart, and lean not on your own understanding; in all your ways acknowledge Him, and He shall direct your paths.

What do we lean upon? We can't just exist; we must be both spirit and natural and dwell with God in our lives. We must embrace our lives and know that God is in agreement with our lives as well. He wants to direct our paths. He wants to give us good thoughts, good reasoning, good emotions, and good desires. When we attach our spirits to the Spirit of God within us we can trust our thoughts, reasoning, emotions, and desires. These expressions of our souls will not be bent towards pleasing ourselves, but they will be impassioned to love God and to live for the wellbeing of others. I cannot express how important it is to embrace how God is revealed in Scripture in this process. The Scripture is not our teacher, but the Scripture is a written witness to the One who teaches our hearts. The Holy Spirit inspired the Scripture; therefore, the Scripture is also a witness to the voice of the Holy Spirit. The Holy Spirit inspired the Scripture, but it is filled with statements of truth and truly-stated statements. When looked at in its context and entirety, it reveals the truth of God. It is a witness to the failures of humanity and the redemption of God among men. Knowing God's word will help us recognize His voice when He speaks. If we don't know the kind of things He says, we are apt to fall for the deception of other voices that promote the strength of our own will and kingdoms.

Psalms 37:3-6 Trust in the LORD, and do good; Dwell in the land, and feed on His faithfulness. Delight yourself also in the LORD, And He shall give you the desires of your heart. Commit your way to the LORD, trust also in Him, and He shall bring it to pass. He shall bring forth your righteousness as the light, and your justice as the noonday.

The heart is the full you – spirit, soul, and body. If God has your heart He has to have all of you. A good man is a warring, passionate man. A good man is virtuous in character. He desires to please God and to give his life for the wellbeing of others. Spirit to spirit is the link of the heart, but my feet had better respond. If God has my heart, my wallet will respond. If God has my heart, my actions will be acts of faith demonstrating my love for God and my love for people. The heart supplies blood to every tributary of your body. Your complexion will reflect your heart. If your heart is right you can miss hearing God, yet not miss it in Him. He will even intervene in the areas of your mistakes if He has all of your heart. It would be different if God had gotten through to you and then you rebelled.

Psalms 37:23-24 The steps of a good man are ordered by the LORD, and He delights in his way. Though he fall, he shall not be utterly cast down; for the LORD upholds him with His hand.

When God speaks to our spirits, it affects our souls. It will even affect our flesh. The flesh contains our five senses. Is there anything wrong with our five senses? There is nothing wrong with our flesh. It is simply not what leads us in life. We walk according to the Spirit, not the flesh. We do walk, however. The realm of the spirit can affect our senses. At times I have angels that work with me in my ministry in Christ. When these angels appear I sense them in my senses. I even experience physical responses to their presence. The same happens when God reveals His presence to me. At times I have smelled the fragrance of God. There is a specific scent when He comes with healing. There is a special fragrance with His desire for intimacy. On one occasion He released the smell of earth as a witness of His love for humanity. There is even a smell when the enemy is present. We can expect to experience God in our lives in our spirits, souls, and bodies. These things work together in defining His voice, His presence, and His will in our lives.

Hearing God is a matter of relationship with God. We can trust His love, because we can trust who He is in our lives.

2. God's Method of Establishing His Will For Our Lives

The human heart is the core of every man and woman and it is spirit. Its substance came from God and it is the place of connection with God for every man and woman. God's voice comes first to our spirits. Though the human heart is spirit, a healthy heart is seen through the countenance of the soul and expressed in the actions of every human life. The essence of being a human being involves the substance of spirit, soul, and body. In order for a man or a woman to fulfill their destiny in life, they must learn how to unite their spirit, soul, and body to God's will and way in their lives. Religion seeks to separate the spirit, soul, and body from one another, often calling the spirit good, the soul soulish, and the body carnal and of no great value. I have addressed these things previously, and I believe that this type of thinking is destructive to human destiny. God want's to unite our spirit, soul, and body for His glory. It is only when we embrace the unity of our spirit, soul, and body that we fulfill our full purpose in life.

The highest form of communication is the Holy Spirit speaking to the human heart. God speaks to our spirit, but it brings a response to our soul and to our flesh. When we receive a prophecy we hear it with our ears, see it with our natural eyes, and experience it with our natural senses in some way. Although we experience what is being expressed to us in some natural way, we have to receive it with our spirit and witness it with Christ's Spirit within us. God is Spirit so in order to hear God we must hear Him with our spirit. This is the first place of hearing God. It is not our soul. Our soul is the second place of hearing in our lives, but we don't hear God with our soul. We hear our spirit from within as it is empowered by God's Holy Spirit. It is not beneficial to attempt to hear God with our soul. We must learn to submit our soul to what we witness with our spirit. We must also learn to connect our physical actions and expressions with our soul, once our soul has been empowered by our spirit within. The source of it all is Christ in us. The voice of the Holy Spirit in the human heart is the source of legitimate hearing for every human being.

How can we aid this process? There are practical things that we can do in the process of hearing God. Have you ever tried to build one of those particleboard projects, such as a piece of furniture that you must assemble yourself? If you don't take the time to read the instructions, you usually lose some parts, break some parts, or simply become frustrated in your attempts to assemble the thing. I, for one, hate reading those instruction papers, but I do find that the project is much more efficient if I do. It is the same way in the process of hearing God. Sometimes we have to embrace some things that our soul doesn't like in order to complete the process of hearing God correctly. Remember, hearing God is more about becoming than it is about doing something for God. Children don't approach their parents for instructions alone. Most of the time they approach their parents for love and identity in the family. Parents don't desire to merely be teachers of good to their children. They approach them as the ones who love them and want them to become all that they are meant to be. Our relationship with God should be the same. Think of hearing God as a part of your family relationship with God. Most of the time your conversations are not about what to do. They are simply connections of intimacy as a family. We must remember this when talking about the practical actions we can take to assist us in hearing God.

We must remember that God's voice always brings faith. Faith doesn't initiate in the soul. It initiates from the spirit and then your spirit floods your soul. This is when the voice of God begins to take on thoughts, reasoning, imagination, and emotions that you can understand. This is a process and is only a part the steps to understanding what God is speaking in your heart. Faith comes to us when God speaks to our hearts.

Romans 10:17 So then faith comes by hearing, and hearing by the word of God.

When we hear God it empowers us to respond to Him with thoughts that are inspired by our spirit within. I believe that the New Covenant expression of praying in the Spirit, praying in tongues, is a huge thing in our process of hearing God. Praying in the spirit is more powerful than the thoughts that come to our heads from any outside source. Praying in the Spirit stirs up the voice of God in our hearts and allows us to hear God. Faith doesn't come by praying in the Spirit. Faith comes when we hear God in our hearts, but praying in the Spirit can silence the outside voices to our souls by the rising inspiration of God's voice to our hearts. It allows a fresh Spirit-to-spirit word to come into our inner being.

Jude 1:17-21 But you, beloved, remember the words which were spoken before by the apostles of our Lord Jesus Christ: how they told you that there would be mockers in the last time who would walk according to their own ungodly lusts. These are sensual persons, who cause divisions, not having the Spirit. But you, beloved, building yourselves up on your most holy faith, praying in the Holy Spirit, keep yourselves in the love of God, looking for the mercy of our Lord Jesus Christ unto eternal life.

Sensual people are people who are led by their natural senses. These sensual people didn't feel good about you. They didn't perceive what they saw you doing as being good. These sensual people didn't naturally understand you so with what they perceived to be good intentions, not God intentions, they spoke evil of you. Now you are naturally hearing what they are saying about you. You could respond to what is entering your soul gate from an outside source, but that would make you no different than them. When this happens you must respond to the spirit gate not the ear gate, eye gate, or any feeling gate. You must position your spirit to hear His word. Praying in the Spirit is a practical way of stirring up your spirit to hear God's voice in your heart. It comes from within you. A prosperous spirit will produce a prosperous soul and will manifest as a prosperous life.

3 John 2 Beloved, I pray that you may prosper in all things and be in health, just as your soul prospers.

God's voice brings instructions of God's will for your life. These instructions come as revelation to your soul. Your eyes haven't seen, heard, nor your mind thought it, but God is revealing things to you in your spirit. You must learn to never allow your natural man to be a stronger voice than the spirit man within you. You must submit your soul to the voice of your heart, once the heart of God within you has inspired your heart. Your body responds to your soul when your soul connects to your spirit.

God's instructions carry the power of transformation and do not merely bring information. When God speaks to our spirits we begin to be changed in the expression of our souls. God's thoughts sound like our thoughts. His desires actually become our desires. All of a sudden we desire what He desires. It affects our imagination and we begin to receive a whole thought-process filled with strategy and understanding that is the will of God being made real in our hearts and in our minds. When we receive God's word, Spirit to spirit, it floods our souls and changes our lives and the actions of our lives.

Hebrews 8:10-11 "For this is the covenant that I will make with the house of Israel: After those days, says the Lord, I will put My laws in their mind and write them on their hearts; and I will be their God, and they shall be My people. None of them shall teach his neighbor, and none his brother, saying, 'Know the Lord,' for all shall know Me, from the least of them to the greatest of them."

Hearing God is about knowing God, not merely about knowing what to do in life. We hear God in our hearts and it is in our hearts that we come to know Him intimately. We must allow God's Spirit to activate our spirits within in order to increasingly understand in our souls His will in our lives.

3. Identifying God's Will

1 Peter 1:6-9 In this you greatly rejoice, though now for a little while, if need be, you have been grieved by various trials, that the genuineness of your faith, being much more precious than gold that perishes, though it is tested by fire, may be found to praise, honor, and glory at the revelation of Jesus Christ, whom having not seen you love. Though now you do not see Him, yet believing, you rejoice with joy inexpressible and full of glory, receiving the end of your faith – the salvation of your souls.

God is faithful in the midst of all things. God wants us to know Him and His power that sustains us in life. These verses are not talking about a revelation about Jesus, but a revelation of Jesus in our hearts. When we receive a revelation of Jesus Christ within our hearts, we experience life in our thoughts, reasoning, imaginations, emotions and desires. Our souls becomes flooded and energized by that which comes to our spirits. The testimony of our faith is the salvation of our souls in all things.

1 Peter 1:13-16 Therefore gird up the loins of your mind, be sober, and rest your hope fully upon the grace that is to be brought to you at the revelation of Jesus Christ; as obedient children, not conforming yourselves to the former lusts, as in your ignorance; but as He who called you is holy, you also be holy in all your conduct, because it is written, "Be holy, for I am holy."

Hearing God in our hearts is essential life-giving change in our lives.

Hearing God reveals His mercy and brings us into His grace. Grace is the power to change our lives. Grace is the substance of God's presence in our lives. Grace comes at a revealing of Christ in us. The key is how we think. We must submit our souls to our spirits once we connect our spirits to God's Holy Spirit. The beginning comes by experiencing His transformation in our hearts. We experience a change within that causes us to become what God desires for us to be. We cannot do the will of God without being the will of God. Hearing God allows us to become the substance of the will of God – spirit, soul, and body.

Hearing God is not about receiving the right information in life. It is about being empowered for the right transformation in life. Much information can bring much confusion. God's instructions bring the power of transformation, thus they empower the hearer to do and become. This doesn't mean that we don't have to do anything in order to hear. Sometimes we have to position ourselves to do in order to hear. This is why it is so important that we learn what the general will of God is in our lives. When we choose to stand in obedience to God's general will, we hear His specific will in our hearts. When we position ourselves to do, we become. This is the proving ground for hearing God and the power of His grace at work in our lives. We do not become something by doing things, but standing to do positions us for the miracle of God's voice in our hearts.

Romans 5:1-5 Therefore, having been justified by faith, we have peace with God through our Lord Jesus Christ, through whom also we have access by faith into this grace in which we stand, and rejoice in hope of the glory of God. And not only that, but we also glory in tribulations, knowing that tribulation produces perseverance; and perseverance, character; and character, hope. Now hope does not disappoint, because the love of God has been poured out in our hearts by the Holy Spirit who was given to us.

Hearing God produces faith in our hearts. There is no gap between us and God. We can hear Him in our hearts. When we hear Him we receive a revelation of Jesus Christ in our inner being and God grants

145

us the power of His grace. The proving ground of God's grace is the tribulation that comes against us. When we experience the pressure or the testing of life we find ourselves persevering. It is not a matter of disciplining the flesh. It is a matter of revealing the power of Christ within us. Perseverance is a joyful endurance that comes from the voice of God in our hearts. This is the testimony that proves to manifest the character of Christ within us and this is seen as our hope of glory. It is our hope of change that comes from within when we hear God's voice. The testimony is for our full being. God's will is for the salvation of our whole man.

1 Thessalonians 5:23 Now may the God of peace Himself sanctify you completely; and may your whole spirit, soul, and body be preserved blameless at the coming of our Lord Jesus Christ.

We can't hate the flesh, beat up on the soul, and pursue the Spirit. We must pursue the Spirit, delight the soul in Him, and present our body as a living sacrifice to God. Hearing God affects all of our being.

What is the will of God in our lives? I believe that God's will in any situation is salvation in that situation. Salvation is not just the testimony of going to heaven when we die. It is a continual process and it includes the testimony of the life of God in any situation in life. Eternal life is to know God and Jesus Christ whom He sent. This is a daily reality. Salvation is the power of eternal life in the testimony of our lives. God is constantly working things out in our lives.

Romans 8:28 And we know that all things work together for good to those who love God, to those who are the called according to His purpose.

O my goodness! I thought I was getting out of the situation! But in order for God to work things out I must find Him in the situations of my life. It isn't a matter of me escaping my daily circumstances.

God wants to move into our worlds with us. That might change the situation, but it is not intended to just get us out of it. If we don't love God, it might not work out for us. We must position ourselves to hear God in order to stand in faith. Salvation is experiencing God in the situation. How you leave a thing is how you enter the next. We must know how to stand and where to stand in order to be in the right place at the right time for the will of God to work out in our lives. If we know God's will we can have God's salvation.

How would we know God's will? We must forget about 'what to do' and simply connect ourselves to Him as a matter of relationship. He is our Father and we are His children. When we depend upon Him, we can trust Him. Knowing the will of God begins by allowing Him to fill our spirits with the life of His Spirit. The will of God comes from the place of desire and faith. These things can only be birthed in the human spirit. When we receive the life of God's Spirit in our spirits it carries the power of transformation.

Chapter 12

Knowing God's Will

1. How do We Know God's Will?

How do we know the will of God in our lives? The fruit of God's Spirit in our lives reveals the will of God. God's will in our lives always produces life in us and that life will be life to those around us. It is a testimony of the fruit of eternal life, a life-giving relationship with God and Father and Jesus His Son through the life of Holy Spirit. A personal relationship with God produces the fruit of that relationship. The will of God in our lives is a fruit of relationship with God. We cannot make fruit. It pops out! There can be no wooden or wax fruit in the testimony of the will of God in our lives. Fruit is not something we create. Fruit is a testimony of life. We can't pretend to be in the will of God and think that it is enough. There is not fruit of life in lifeless efforts. We can't take fruit and throw it at a tree and make it stick. To be alive it must be the natural result of life within the tree. How do we know God's will in our lives?

Ephesians 5:8-10 For you were once darkness, but now you are light in the Lord. Walk as children of light (for the fruit of the Spirit is in all goodness, righteousness, and truth), finding out what is acceptable to the Lord.

The context of Ephesians chapter 5 is walking in the light. It is about walking in love. If we walk as children of God, the things of darkness should not be among us. The Textus Receptus version of the Greek uses the word *pneuma* or *Spirit* in verse 9, while other early

Greek texts use the word *phos* or *Light*. The New American Standard Bible reads:

Ephesians 5:9 ...(for the fruit of the Light consists in all goodness and righteousness and truth)...

When this word is used the word *consists* was added to the text to imply that the fruit of Light is goodness, righteousness, and truth. The Textus Receptus Greek says that the fruit of the Spirit is in all goodness, righteousness, and truth. I like this better, simply because I have found that I don't always properly discern what is good, or righteous, or true. I believe that the fruit of the Spirit is the evidence of discovering what is good, righteous, and true. If what I am doing does not manifest the attributes of love, joy, peace, longsuffering, kindness, goodness, faithfulness, gentleness, and self-control it cannot be righteous, good or true.

If the fruit of the Spirit is not evident in our lives, then there is something that needs to be adjusted in our way. I find this true in my own life. When something is good, righteous, or true the fruit of the Spirit is present. I have experienced many times where I thought something was good, or righteous, or true, but the fruit of the Holy Spirit was not there. I found myself to be anxious, frustrated, self-focused, or self-gratifying in some way. In the process of my journey I found that what I thought was good was not good. I found that what I thought was righteous was self-righteousness and it lacked the righteousness of relationship or dependency upon God and others. I found that what I thought was truth was my own opinion, misinterpretation of God's words, or a deception promoted by the traditions of men.

Sometimes we fail to understand what is good, righteous, or true. We must change our thinking, we cannot expect God to redefine His definitions for these things when they don't agree with what we want or what we think is right.

The will of God is not revealed through our own way. It is revealed through the way of God being known in our lives. When we seek our own will in a matter we end up expressing foolish talk. Complaining and murmuring could be foolish talking. Children accusing parents of not loving them are merely expressing thoughts of foolishness. We must stop our foolish talking in order to find the will of God in our lives! This is another reason we must seek to know the general will of God by finding His character, nature, way, power, and authority in His written word. We must seek to know who He is in order to discern the kinds of things He says and does.

When my children were little my wife and I taught them how to change a bad attitude to a good one and to 'happy up'. If they were not manifesting the fruit of the Spirit in some way, we would instruct them to fold their hands and to take charge of their spirit. We would say, "I want you to happy up." We discovered that it is possible to find 'happy' in our hearts and let it manifest. This worked quite well in raising our children and they all turned out to be very happy adults. We must all know how to join our spirits to the Spirit of God. We must all learn how to attach our hearts to the truth. We must all learn to allow our spirits to flood our souls with right thoughts, emotions, and desires when we attach our spirits to the Spirit of God in our hearts. When we do these things, the fruit of the Spirit will manifest. If the fruit of the Spirit is not there, something is not quite right.

The peace of God is an evidence of God's will. Peace is the testimony of being one with God. If we don't have peace, something is missing in the will of God in our lives. We must learn to listen for the peace of God in our hearts. Peace is the evidence of being one with God. It is the place of no separation between God and us.

Philippians 4:6-7 Be anxious for nothing, but in everything by prayer and supplication, with thanksgiving, let your requests be made known to God; and the peace of God, which surpasses all understanding, will guard your hearts and minds through Christ Jesus.

Peace is the place of no separation between God and us. It is not the absence of conflict. It is an inner knowing that there is no separation between God and us. If we seek to do something but we feel a hesitation in our hearts when we do, it is a check to the peace of God in our hearts. Something is not quite right in some way and we must trust the peace or the lack of peace in our hearts to discern what God is saying. The will of God is always witnessed by a release in our hearts.

1 John 3:19-24 And by this we know that we are of the truth, and shall assure our hearts before Him. For if our heart condemns us, God is greater than our heart, and knows all things. Beloved, if our heart does not condemn us, we have confidence toward God. And whatever we ask we receive from Him, because we keep His commandments and do those things that are pleasing in His sight. And this is His commandment: that we should believe on the name of His Son Jesus Christ and love one another, as He gave us commandment. Now he who keeps His commandments abides in Him, and He in him. And by this we know that He abides in us, by the Spirit whom He has given us.

The will of God is absent condemnation. Confidence is the opposite of condemnation. A confidence to respond to what God says is different than a condemnation to do what we think He says. God's words in our hearts do not put shame upon our lives. His words bring release into our hearts. God's words in us promote a confidence to respond to Him with an attitude of faith and a testimony of life from within. When something is not the will of God we almost always know it in our hearts. We then begin to talk ourselves into or out of something we already know to be the will of God. We know it in our hearts, but our minds are trying to reason some other way. A good question to ask is: "What is my heart telling me?"

2. Reaching The Knowing Stage of His Will

The will of God affects our spirits, souls, and our bodies. God's will in our lives doesn't have to make us miserable. It doesn't have to always promote immediate happiness either. God's full conclusion of

His will in our lives is always meant to bring to pass good for others. It is good for us, but even more it is good to others because of us. Even if we were to be martyred for Christ, the immediate testimony will be our good in heaven and in the long term it will be someone else's good upon the earth. Misery doesn't mean we are out of the will of God, but it is not the goal either. In sickness the will of God is righteousness, peace, and joy in the process. In health the will of God is righteousness, peace, and joy. Living in God, moving in God, and having our being in Him is always the will of God in every situation in life. If we find ourselves in a day of sickness, the practical working of God's will for our lives could be a supernatural healing. God could use the process of hospitals, doctors, and nurses in sharing our journey of righteousness, peace, and joy in the Holy Spirit with the lives we touch. We could be an example of faith to others. We are the testimony of God. It is not just the supernatural miracles that testify of His goodness. The process of doctors and medicine could lead us to a recovery and a testimony of returning home. We could even end up dying and experience a promotion to heaven beyond this life. Sick people are not necessarily out of the will of God. Healthy people are not necessarily in the will of God. Destiny is a journey. We must always stand in the place of God's grace to drink the cup that life gives us to drink. Life is not fair, but God is good in the midst of all things.

In finding the will of God in our lives, the source of the will of God is the Spirit of God. Coming to the knowing stage of the will of God in our lives is simply the fruit of a personal relationship with God. It is made known through our relationship of being one with Him. It is not naturally understood (1 Cor. 2:1-7). It is first understood in our hearts.

In discovering His will and walking in that process, we must forget asking 'why' and accept the fact we might not understand. A two-year old child might ask the questions of why, but at some point we must grow beyond the place of always having to know the why of something. I believe that much of the body of Christ approaches the will of God from the terrible 2's with the question, "Why?"

1 Corinthians 2:1-7 And I, brethren, when I came to you, did not come with excellence of speech or of wisdom declaring to you the testimony of God. For I determined not to know anything among you except Jesus Christ and Him crucified. I was with you in weakness, in fear, and in much trembling. And my speech and my preaching were not with persuasive words of human wisdom, but in demonstration of the Spirit and of power, that your faith should not be in the wisdom of men but in the power of God. However, we speak wisdom among those who are mature, yet not the wisdom of this age, nor of the rulers of this age, who are coming to nothing. But we speak the wisdom of God in a mystery, the hidden wisdom which God ordained before the ages for our glory...

Our faith is not in the wisdom of men. It is in the power of God. The will of God in our lives is a supernatural will. It can only be possible by the working of the power of the Holy Spirit in our lives. We must come to the place of maturity, beyond our natural man. We must embrace the wisdom of God that is revealed to our inner man by Christ at work in our hearts. It is there that we find the testimony of divine love and faith. When we find the will of God in our hearts we find that it also floods our souls from within.

Our soul is the area of our emotions, reasoning, imaginations, and our desires. Nothing is wrong with these things, but the Spirit in our lives must be the motivator of them all. Our emotions, reasoning, imaginations, and desires are in fact a gift from God to make the things of God visible to the world in which we live. For this to happen, we need a different motivation than our own understanding. Having no motivation is apathy. We do not want to be dead in our emotions, reasoning, imaginations, or desires. The will of God has a motivation. Desire will be birthed within. It is a gift given to us by the mystery Christ in us, so our souls will prosper and we can tangibly express life-giving authority through the actions of our lives. The will of God is more than a decision, but it starts with a decision in our hearts that motivates a decision in our souls. This is then expressed in our lives. All of these are expressions of life. A desire will come from within that becomes visible in our souls and it will be seen in the workings of our lives.

Revelation 3:15-18 "I know your works, that you are neither cold nor hot. I could wish you were cold or hot. So then, because you are lukewarm, and neither cold nor hot, I will vomit you out of My mouth. Because you say, 'I am rich, have become wealthy, and have need of nothing'– and do not know that you are wretched, miserable, poor, blind, and naked – I counsel you to buy from Me gold refined in the fire, that you may be rich; and white garments, that you may be clothed, that the shame of your nakedness may not be revealed; and anoint your eyes with eye salve, that you may see."

True gold refined in the fire is the testimony of the faithfulness of God in our hearts. It is a passion within our hearts that is tested faith that becomes faith-FULL.

Revelation 3:20 "Behold, I stand at the door and knock. If anyone hears My voice and opens the door, I will come in to him and dine with him, and he with Me."

What happens to our emotions, reasoning, imaginations, and desires when He comes into our hearts? When the Spirit of God floods our hearts these things become transformed from being self-focused to God-focused and life-giving to others. The will of God in our lives will be marked with a motivation to love God and others. For this to happen, we may have to position ourselves to receive the will before we know we are in the will of God. This is where knowing the general will of God is essential. The receiving of God's will is in our hearts, but the frequency of God's voice is the character, nature, and way of His heart.

Every human soul is inspired by the influence of the realm of the spirit. When our own spirit is empowered by the Spirit of Christ within our hearts we receive God's life-giving influence to our souls. This is the foundation for being a healthy person in life. A healthy spirit will produce a healthy soul and this is key to living a healthy life. When our spirit is not empowered by the Holy Spirit we are tempted to allow our soul to be influenced by our own natural understanding. This then causes our own senses to become self-focused and self-motivated. It can lead to strong personal opinions of self-preservation. When this happens our soul becomes vulnerable to the influence of other spirits from an outside source.

James 3:14-15 But if you have bitter envy and self-seeking in your hearts, do not boast and lie against the truth. This wisdom does not descend from above, but is earthly, sensual, and demonic.

Spirit motivations influence the soul's emotions, reasoning, imaginations, and desires. Any spirit will motivate a soul. This is why the enemy, who is also spirit, wars against our souls (1 Pet. 2:11). He wars against the thrones of our lives that are filled with reasoning, imagination, emotions, and desires. God desires to motivate these realities of our souls with His Spirit in the power of our lives. The power of our lives is our hearts. They are only motivated by life when the Holy Spirit within each of us motivates them. God's Spirit will motivate our spirits and then our spirits flood our souls with His life. The key to life of the soul is a life giving Spirit. The Holy Spirit!

John 6:63 "It is the Spirit who gives life; the flesh profits nothing. The words that I speak to you are spirit, and they are life."

2 Corinthians 3:5-6 Not that we are sufficient of ourselves to think of anything as being from ourselves, but our sufficiency is from God, who also made us sufficient as ministers of the new covenant, not of the letter but of the Spirit; for the letter kills, but the Spirit gives life.

Only one Spirit gives life and that Spirit will motivate our souls to be filled with life-giving thoughts, imaginations, emotions, and desires. Christ in us is the hope of Glory. It comes from within.

1 Corinthians 15:45 And so it is written, "The first man Adam became a living being." The last Adam became a life-giving spirit.

As I have stated, the flesh contains our five senses. There is nothing wrong with the five senses, but they are not the gates to knowing the will of God. They can serve a role in the 'big picture'. We live in the flesh, but we do not walk according to the flesh. We should 'live in the flesh,' but not according to the flesh. We must choose to live according to the Spirit while still walking out our lives in natural and practical ways. The senses serve the soul that serves the spirit. We must learn to walk in the maturity of submission to one another in the makeup of our being. We are spirit, soul, and body and these things are one. Natural things are part of the process as well. Some things don't require direction from the Spirit. Some things are a natural will. We should know not to touch a hot stove once we have learned that a stove is hot. Practical things are not less important than things that must be discerned by the Spirit. We are spiritual in our being and this includes things which are spirit and things which are natural.

Our authority as a person is based upon a submission of receiving and giving. There must be a submission of our soul to our spirit, but we are not led by our soul. We are led by our spirits that are empowered by God's Spirit within. We must learn to walk with submission of our senses to our souls, but we are not led by senses. They are merely contributing factors to the discernment of our decision making process in life.

The will of God will fall within your responsibilities. God's will is revealed in our lives according to who each of us is. God's voice will pertain to us as a parent to our children, a spouse to our spouses, an employee to our employers. Being a parent doesn't make us a parent to other parents' children, a spouse to another person's spouse, or an employer to our employer, or an employee of some other company in town. The will of God will not make us irresponsible. His voice will always lead us toward being responsible for who we are and it will never endorse irresponsibility in our lives. A voice that leads to irresponsibility is a voice that is not the voice of God. If it sounds like God, it is merely an enemy in disguise.

God's voice in our lives is a voice of wisdom. The wisdom of God is a spiritual wisdom, not a human wisdom. It is a voice of faith, not natural understanding. It is the sound of God's wisdom and it often concerns things we haven't seen, heard, or thought before. Wisdom is a direction for the future. The future of God is a place of increasing life. His voice can include a word of knowledge, but we must remember it is only a word. It is not all knowledge. It may include a word of wisdom, but we must remember it is also only a word. It is not all wisdom. The will of God can include an equation: wisdom + knowledge = understanding. The will of God is not an event. It is a process. The will of God is staying in the place of intimacy with Him that leads to words of knowledge and words of wisdom. By this we continually walk in understanding. Who we are in the journey is the point. The will of God comes by hearing His voice and we are the will of God. It is the testimony of being the place of intimacy with God in the earth.

3. Your Spirit is the Key to Hearing God

When it comes to hearing God, our spirits are the key to discerning His voice. Another word for this is 'heart'. Our hearts are the secret place where the voice of God is heard from within. When we hear God in our hearts it causes our minds to become alive with the thoughts of God. Thoughts come before reasoning in the gate of heaven. The gate of heaven is the human heart, not the human head. Reasoning is in the mind, not the spirit. Reasoning is not bad. Thinking is a good thing to do, but we must learn how to get good reasoning in our minds. Strongholds in our hearts create strongholds in our minds. We need the stronger hold of God's love and life to be conceived in our hearts. This is the key to receiving the thoughts of God in our minds.

Colossians 1:21 And you, who once were alienated and enemies in your mind by wicked works, yet now He has reconciled.

No one needs to be an enemy of God. God wants to grant us all the gift of repentance in our hearts. This is the gift of God's desire birthed in our hearts. When this happens we become empowered to receive a change in our thinking. We change our minds because of His mercy and great grace.

Our traditions, beliefs, and strong opinions are not a true witness to the will of God. Traditions aren't necessarily bad. Beliefs aren't bad. Strong opinions are not necessarily bad. They are simply not a good witness. Traditions can help preserve what God has done, but our traditions must not stop God from doing new things in our lives. Sometimes instructions from God in the past can become hindrances to God's voice in our present. When the children of Israel complained against God and Moses, serpents came among them and began to bite them. God instructed Moses to make a bronze (brass) serpent and lift it on a pole before the people. This was a symbol of the death of Jesus upon the cross for our sins. It was a testimony of Jesus's death for the judgment of sin. When the people looked at the serpent on the pole the poisonous bites were healed.

Numbers 21:8-9 Then the LORD said to Moses, "Make a fiery serpent, and set it on a pole; and it shall be that everyone who is bitten, when he looks at it, shall live." So Moses made a bronze serpent, and put it on a pole; and so it was, if a serpent had bitten anyone, when he looked at the bronze serpent, he lived.

The people kept the brass serpent and it became a symbol of worship upon the high place, many generations past the day of God's instruction to Moses. God sent King Hezekiah to tear it down, because it had become a thing of judgment, a thing of brass (a symbol of judgment), among the people..

2 Kings 18:4 He removed the high places and broke the sacred pillars, cut down the wooden image and broke in pieces the bronze serpent that Moses had made; for until those days the children of Israel burned incense to it, and called it Nehushtan.

Traditions can stop what God wants to do in our lives. Traditions, beliefs, and strong opinions often bring doubt, confusion, resentment, rejection, and rebellion towards the will of God. We must remember the will of God is witnessed by the peace that surpasses understanding. Our minds' understanding is not the witness of God's will.

I believe that every aspect of the church carries strength. The word Catholic, means 'universal' and it is a testimony to a kingdom mindset in the traditions of the Catholic church. They saw themselves as the universal church, and thus they built things to last for generations. If you ask a Catholic if they are a Christian, their likely response will be that they are a Catholic. They have a strong sense of belonging to something that is global. When God begins to challenge a Catholic with new things concerning believing, they can sometimes be hindered by their inherited tradition of belonging. The traditions of their works can sometimes hinder them from simply trusting faith and God's love.

Presbyterians have a great sense of God and His kingdom. They can have a great kingdom theology, but may be resistant to things of the manifest presence of Christ's Spirit. Baptism by submersion can be resisted by their thinking of sprinkling babies as an act of faith to embrace the Presbyterian faith. Water baptism as an act of faith towards God by complete submersion in water could be resisted because of their Presbyterian tradition.

Baptists can pride themselves in studying the word of God, but sometimes their strong hold to God's word through their traditional perceptions can resist the testimony of the power and presence of the Holy Spirit today. Everyone of us have traditions in our past that will hinder God's voice in our present through the strongholds of the thinking in our minds.

Have you noticed that when God gives revelation the very Scriptures you used to defend your beliefs become the fuel of your fresh new revelation? I have found this to be true in my life on many occasions. When I allow God's voice in the present to be more powerful than my understanding of His voice in the past I find new faith to see new things in the very place of what I thought was truth.

We often confuse a negative soul reaction with the Spirit's lack of witness to something. We must not confuse the soul realm with the Spirit. We have to learn to attach our souls to our spirits after we attach our spirits to God's Spirit. Past revelations can become a high place. They sound like the voice of God. We must let God be Lord, or our 'want to' not merely the 'what to' in our lives. Blind spots in our vision make us blind. Deceptions in our thinking are deceiving. Religious comfort zones entice us to be reluctant to pursue the fresh things of God in our lives. Our souls can resist the will of God in our lives, but we must trust the peace of our hearts within, more than the turmoil of our souls. This is why Jesus could embrace the will of His Father in the garden before His crucifixion (Lk. 22:41-42). He knew the secret to the voice of God was in His heart, not His head. This enabled Him to embrace the will of God in His heart.

4. Finding God's Direction and Wisdom

Embracing the will of God will lead us into the things of God in our lives. God wants to lead us into things that are beyond anything that we have known before. How can we acquire God's wisdom and direction for our future? We must first know that God's thoughts are always for our future and they are thoughts of hope, even if circumstances don't communicate this to us. At the beginning of Israel's seventy years of captivity, God spoke through the prophet Jeremiah that His thoughts for them were thoughts of a future and a hope (Jer. 29:11). We must remember that our natural man does not receive the things of the Spirit of God, so we must put our natural man into subjection to our inner spirit man in an environment of embracing the manifest presence of Christ.

1 Corinthians 2:9-16 But as it is written: "Eye has not seen, nor ear heard, nor have entered into the heart of man the things which God has prepared for those who love Him." But God has revealed them to us through His Spirit. For the Spirit searches all things, yes, the deep things of God. For what man knows the things of a man except the spirit of the man which is in him? Even so no one knows the things of God except the Spirit of God. Now we have received, not the spirit of the world, but the Spirit who is from God, that we might know the things that have been freely given to us by God. These things we also speak, not in words which man's wisdom teaches but which the Holy Spirit teaches, comparing spiritual things with spiritual. But the natural man does not receive the things of the Spirit of God, for they are foolishness to him; nor can he know them, because they are spiritually discerned. But he who is spiritual judges all things, yet he himself is rightly judged by no one. For "who has known the mind of the Lord that he may instruct Him?" But we have the mind of Christ.

We must tell our natural man, "You are natural. Don't judge things by what you see, hear, or think right now." We must always subject our natural man to the Spirit. We must be careful. Our thoughts might not be right. What we are seeing might not be what we think. What we are hearing might not be totally accurate.

We must never debate with our natural man. The natural man is not bad. Part of us is a natural man or woman. It is the part of us that simply cannot receive the things of God on its own. The natural man is not necessarily the flesh led man. It has the potential of walking according to the flesh or according to the Spirit. We are sojourners both natural and spirit, thus we are spiritual. We are natural, but the Spirit must always lead us.

1 Peter 1:17 And if you call on the Father, who without partiality judges according to each one's work, conduct yourselves throughout the time of your stay here in fear...

Only our spirit man can receive the things of God. Our natural man cannot receive the things of God without submitting to our spirit man. God wants us to experience what we cannot receive naturally. We need a supernatural relationship with God. We need both natural bread and Living Bread to be healthy people.

Romans 8:5-8 For those who live according to the flesh set their minds on the things of the flesh, but those who live according to the Spirit, the things of the Spirit. For to be carnally minded is death, but to be spiritually minded is life and peace. Because the carnal mind is enmity against God; for it is not subject to the law of God, nor indeed can be. So then, those who are in the flesh cannot please God.

Being spiritual is not being a spiritual spook. Pursuing the things of the Spirit is not pursuing an out-of-body experience with God. It is pursuing the Spirit of Christ through our hearts that empowers our spirits, souls, and bodies to be one before Him. We cannot exalt one part of our being and consider this a sign of maturity. Our spirits, souls, and bodies are all one before Him and the voice of God is meant to empower our full being to be led by Him. We are led by the Spirit of Christ in our spirits, impassioned in our souls by the passion of our spirits from within, and this is expressed in our lives in natural ways through the outward testimony of who we are in this world. The flesh does not lead us; the Spirit leads us. We do walk in the flesh, but the inspiration of our foot steps comes by the Spirit of Christ within us. We are not walking according to our own carnal desires.

Romans 8:26-28 Likewise the Spirit also helps in our weaknesses. For we do not know what we should pray for as we ought, but the Spirit Himself makes intercession for us with groanings which cannot be uttered. Now He who searches the hearts knows what the mind of the Spirit is, because He makes intercession for the saints according to the will of God. And we know that all things work together for good to those who love God, to those who are the called according to His purpose.

We must learn to trust the spirit man within us. Christ in us is the hope of glory, and the Holy Spirit is interceding within our hearts according to the will of God in heaven. We must trust the inner voice of God in our hearts and be lead by Christ's Spirit within us. It is not just trusting a voice; it is trusting the voice of the One who loves us. It is trusting the voice of God's love in our hearts.

We need God's power by God's love at work in our lives. It is not an either/or option. We must pursue practical ways of expressing God's love to others with a supernatural empowerment. There was a time when I was addicted to fasting because my focus was weird. I didn't know how to enjoy life and all of the aspects of life. I thought being spiritual was pursuing only the things of the Spirit. I didn't realize that life is meant to be a testimony of God in every aspect. We must live for God and others.

1 Corinthians 12:31 But earnestly desire the best gifts. And yet I show you a more excellent way.

1 Corinthians 13:1 Though I speak with the tongues of men and of angels, but have not love, I have become sounding brass or a clanging cymbal.

These verses are not saying to stop speaking in the tongues or to stop exercising any other aspect of the power of the Holy Spirit. These verses are simply saying that the love of God towards others is expressed with power. Hearing God's voice is always going to make us spirit-natural. Hearing God will make us responsible people of love.

Our motive in hearing God must be love. Our motive in hearing God is not to make right choices. Our motive in hearing God is not to become spiritual. The motive is to love God and to love others. We should desire to hear God so we can be empowered to love others. It is not a 'what to do', but a 'desire to do'. Hearing God is more about giving than receiving, although it includes receiving. We need God's love and God's gifts.

1 Corinthians 14:1-5 Pursue love, and desire spiritual gifts, but especially that you may prophesy. For he who speaks in a tongue does not speak to men but to God, for no one understands him; however, in the spirit he speaks mysteries. But he who prophesies speaks edification and exhortation and comfort to men. He who speaks in a tongue edifies himself, but he who prophesies edifies the church. I wish you all spoke with tongues, but even more that you prophesied; for he who prophesies is greater than he who speaks with tongues, unless indeed he interprets, that the church may receive edification.

The word for 'pursue' in these verses literally means to 'chase after'. We must 'chase after' every opportunity to show God's love to others. In the Greek this is 'agape' love, the kind of love that makes sacrifices for others and demonstrates those sacrifices with actions of love on their behalf. The word 'desire' means to 'earnestly covet'. We must 'chase' 'after' opportunities to show love to others and we must 'earnestly covet' the supernatural ability of God in doing so. We must 'earnestly covet' to prophesy, to speak Spirit-empowered words of life to others. If we do these things we are doing greater than simply living for the edification of our own lives. The term greater simply means to be larger or more mature; a giver of life to others.

We cannot really show love without the power to love. God's love is a supernatural love.

1 Corinthians 14:14-15 For if I pray in a tongue, my spirit prays, but my understanding is unfruitful. What is the conclusion then? I will pray with the spirit, and I will also pray with the understanding. I will sing with the spirit, and I will also sing with the understanding.

We must embrace the aspect of not understanding, as well as the aspect of understanding, for the sake of others. Hearing God will not only bring life to us, it will bring life to others around us.

The keys to the kingdom of God lie in being able to hear His voice. When we hear God in our hearts it brings righteousness, peace, and joy into our hearts as a witness of the voice of God. These things come when we seek to know God's will, not when we seek to justify our own preconceived ideas about His will.

When Jesus asked His disciples who He was, Peter had a pure revelation by the Holy Spirit that Jesus was the Christ, the Son of the living God (Mt. 16:16-17). Although he had a pure revelation of who Jesus was, he also had preconceived ideas as to what it meant. Our natural man can cause us to have preconceived ideas about the will of God. Peter's natural understanding of the coming kingdom hindered him from recognizing the will of God in the crucifixion of Christ. He had no doubt heard the words of the prophet Daniel and thought he knew what the will of God looked like if Jesus was in fact the Messiah.

Daniel 7:13-14 "I was watching in the night visions, and behold, One like the Son of Man, coming with the clouds of heaven! He came to the Ancient of Days, and they brought Him near before Him. Then to Him was given dominion and glory and a kingdom, that all peoples, nations, and languages should serve Him. His dominion is an everlasting dominion, which shall not pass away, and His kingdom the one which shall not be destroyed."

We don't normally miss God in revelation. It is in the interpretation and application that we are apt to be inaccurate in our ability to hear Him. Revelation from God is usually very easy. Understanding what God is saying to us is another matter. We have preconceived ideas that often cloud the true meaning of His words to us, thus hearing Him with understanding is a process of relationship with Him. We can usually trust the first thing that we hear God say to us, we just can't trust our full understanding of what it means. This was the case with Peter in his perception of Jesus as the Christ.

John 18:1-11 When Jesus had spoken these words, He went out with His disciples over the Brook Kidron, where there was a garden, which He and His disciples entered. And Judas, who betrayed Him, also knew the place; for Jesus often met there with His disciples. Then Judas, having received a detachment of troops, and officers from the chief priests and Pharisees, came there with lanterns, torches, and weapons. Jesus therefore, knowing all things that would come upon Him, went forward and said to them, "Whom are you seeking?" They answered Him, "Jesus of Nazareth." Jesus said to them, "I am He." And Judas, who betrayed Him, also stood with them. Then – when

He said to them, "I am He," – they drew back and fell to the ground. Then He asked them again, "Whom are you seeking?" And they said, "Jesus of Nazareth." Jesus answered, "I have told you that I am He. Therefore, if you seek Me, let these go their way," that the saying might be fulfilled which He spoke, "Of those whom You gave Me I have lost none." Then Simon Peter, having a sword, drew it and struck the high priest's servant, and cut off his right ear. The servant's name was Malchus. So Jesus said to Peter, "Put your sword into the sheath. Shall I not drink the cup which My Father has given Me?"

The will of God for Jesus didn't look like a reigning King, but this was the process that would free all the nations from the bondage of deception. Our own preconceived ideas and personal understanding will hinder us from understanding the true meaning of God's words to us. This is part of the testimony of the power of self and it hinders us in hearing God's voice.

Proverbs 14:12-14 There is a way which seems right to a man, but its end is the way of death. Even in laughter the heart may sorrow, and the end of mirth may be grief. The backslider in heart will be filled with his own ways, but a good man will be satisfied from above.

How do we distinguish the difference between that which comes from outside of the holy of holies and that, which initiates from the place of His presence? We must stay in the place of His presence. We must choose to live with Him in our daily walk in order to get to the place of understanding what He says. We must not just go there, we must live there! If we stay in the place of hearing Him, we will hear and understand what He is saying. It is not a naturally understood place, but a spiritually discerned one. It starts with us presenting our bodies to Him as a living sacrifice (Rom. 12:1). We come to Him and unite our spirits with His Spirit, then we unite our souls with our spirits. When we commit our desires to God He gives us the desires of our hearts. We don't just approach Him or petition Him to know what to do in life. We live with Him and expect Him to be the Lord of our hearts. We live with Him in all things!

We receive revelation from God and then must choose to progress to receiving revelation and interpretation from Him. We must then embrace revelation, interpretation, and application of what He is saying in our lives. It is not simply revelation, then interpretation, and then application. It is a continued process of hearing, hearing and understanding, and hearing, understanding, and walking those things out. This is the process of hearing God made complete. A word from God invites us to continually hear that word in our hearts and begin to discern the will of that word in our lives. This then leads to a continual hearing of the word of God in our hearts, a discerning of His will, and a walking out the practical applications of the way that word and will is being revealed in our lives. The revelation aspect of this process comes from God's Spirit to our spirits. The interpretation process comes when our spirit floods our souls with God's thoughts, reasonings, imaginations, emotions, and desires. The application process comes about through the actions of our lives that are inspired by the thoughts, reasoning, imagination, emotions, and desires of our souls infused by the passions of our hearts from within. A spirit-to-Spirit connection with God in our hearts will lead to revelation or a word from God in our hearts. A proper connection of our souls to our spirits will reveal the righteous desire and will of God in our hearts to cause us to become a testimony of the will of God.

R + (R+I) + (R+I+A) = Hearing Complete
- Revelation = Word
  √ Revelation = Spirit to spirit
- Relation + Interpretation = Will
  √ Revelation + Interpretation = spirit to soul
- Revelation + Interpretation + Application = Way
  √ Revelation + Interpretation + Application = Spirit to spirit to soul to body

Hearing His words, living close to His heart, and responding to His desires leads to an ability to walk out the application of His will in our lives. Righteous interpretation of His voice in our hearts comes through a face-to-face relationship with Him. To know and walk out the will of

God requires us to have heard Him, to hear Him, and be continually hearing Him in our lives. We must seek to know Him more than to know what He has said. The process is a journey of relationship with the One who loves us. It is a journey of love on our part as we embrace the love that He gives on His. If we major on learning God's ways, and not His works, we will be able to hear Him more perfectly.

Psalms 37:23-24 The steps of a good man are ordered by the LORD, And He delights in his way. Though he fall, he shall not be utterly cast down; For the LORD upholds him with His hand.

If we want to know the will of God we must get to know who God is. On the days that we cannot see Him we must look at His emails, His pressed flowers, His poems, and His songs. If we read what He has written and meditate what He has said when we don't hear Him, we will be quick to respond to His voice when He speaks. We must study the expressions He has made to understand the heart of who He is. When we know His ways we will be ready to respond to Him in all that He says.

Psalms 95:10 "For forty years I was grieved with that generation, And said, 'It is a people who go astray in their hearts, And they do not know My ways.'"

We must seek to know God's ways, more than His works. Hearing God and becoming someone who is His will, and walks in His will, means we are people who seek to know His ways. Hearing God is about knowing God, not merely knowing His works. It is a testimony of being those who give Him their hearts and who live from their hearts in knowing Him.

Chapter 13

Questions To Ask

The heart is an amazing thing. Whatever is in our hearts will empower the actions of our lives. If we can keep our hearts right before God, we can keep our hearts open to hearing Him correctly to empower our journeys in life with Him. I want to conclude with a checklist to help us discern our own hearts before God. The purpose of this checklist is not to give us any method or form of law in hearing Him. It is simply given to prompt our minds to consider these things when we believe we are hearing God.

A Check List To Help Discern Your Heart
And Bring Clarity In Hearing God's Voice:

1. Do I know what the full context of the word says so that I can, with complete confidence, say that this is truth?

We must never study the word for facts. We study it to know who God is. We study it for our relationship with Him. The Scripture is not our teacher. The Holy Spirit is our teacher. Without the New Covenant voice of God in our lives, we will read the word of God with an Old Covenant mindset and we will likely misinterpret what it says. A Scripture out of context can lead us into a path of deception. Here is an example of a Scripture that I have heard taken out of context many times.

Proverbs 18:16 A man's gift makes room for him, and brings him before great men.

I have heard this taught that our gifting will make room for us in our places of value in life. I have heard it said that our personal abilities will make room for us before others. This verse has been cited as the reference for such teaching. The word 'gift' in this Scripture is not our own personal abilities that impress others. It is something we give to honor others. When we honor great men we are heard by great men. A good example of this is found in 1 Samuel chapter 25. The story is about David when he had a need and sent for provisions from a rich man named Nabal. Nabal refused to honor David with any provisions. David sent orders to kill Nabal for his dishonor, but Nabal's wife Abigail, met David's men on the road and gave them gifts to honor David on behalf of her wicked husband, Nabal. David received her gifts and decided not to kill Nabal. After David departed Nabal had a heart attack and died ten days later because he didn't honor the authority of God. Abigail gave a gift to honor David and God made room for her in David's house after her husband's death. It was not her personal abilities that made room for her. It was her honor of authority that made room for her in the King's palace. Your abilities don't make room for you, your honor of authority makes room for you before kings.

When we hear God it must be consistent with how God speaks. We study God's word to know what He is like in His character so we won't believe that He says certain things that He would never say.

2. *Am I seeking a work of God or am I seeking His way?*

Why didn't the children of Israel enter the Promised Land? They knew the works of God, but they didn't know His ways.

Psalms 95:10 "For forty years I was grieved with that generation, And said, 'It is a people who go astray in their hearts, And they do not know My ways.'"

3. *Have I sought God's will or God's way on this matter without testing the validity of a word from God first?*

God says that if we don't work, we don't eat. Even if God were to tell us to quit work, it wouldn't be for lack of a job. Our job could be school, ministry, or some form of activity that allows us to serve the betterment of mankind. God will not tell us to be lazy and expect others to provide for us.

2 Thessalonians 3:8 ...nor did we eat anyone's bread free of charge, but worked with labor and toil night and day, that we might not be a burden to any of you...

2 Thessalonians 3:10 For even when we were with you, we commanded you this: If anyone will not work, neither shall he eat.

Proverbs 6:10-11 & 24:33-34 A little sleep, a little slumber, a little folding of the hands to rest; so shall your poverty come like a prowler, and your need like an armed man.

For something to be God's will or way, it must first be legitimate to His character, nature, way, power, and authority. Praying about things that are not true to who He is will only open the door for illegitimate thoughts of deception. Prayers about being in the wrong marriage, should I tithe, should I work, should I lie, should I steal, and other illegitimate requests will only open the door to trouble in our lives.

4. Have I allowed the Holy Spirit to examine the motives of my heart?

Truth is of the Spirit and not the soul. Our mixed up emotions, impure motives, prejudices, preconceived ideas, habit patterns of thought and action, are derived from our souls when they are disconnected from the life-giving power of God's Spirit to our spirits. We must never separate our souls from our spirits. Embracing a face-to-face experience with what God has expressed in the past will pierce through our souls to our spirits and activate the life of God's voice in our hearts (Heb. 4:12). It is a testimony of uniting the spirit to the soul, the life of the marrow to the joint of the bone, and the discernment of thought to the thoughts of our minds. We don't kill our emotions; we make our emotions subject to the emotions of the Spirit. We choose to become God-seeking not self-seeking in our nature, character, way, power and authority.

5. *Is this word or action true to the character and nature of God?*

A voice that says you don't owe money when you do is a voice of deception. A voice that tells you to abandon your commitments when you have made commitments is a voice of deception. If you need a couch and you find one on the road, do you praise God and take it, or do you look to find the owner? Believing that God afflicts men with sickness to teach them a lesson is not true to the character of God as a Father. Thinking that hardship is a teacher is false, while finding the true teacher in the midst of good days or bad is legitimate. The Holy Spirit is the teacher of the hearts and minds of men. Love includes discipline, but the discipline is not the teacher. The heart of the One who loves you is one of covenant character.

6. *Is my motive and desire for seeking God in this matter true to the character and nature of God?*

7. *Is it possible that my emotions may taint my discernment in this area?*

If something irks you, reserve your judgment and keep your mouth shut. If you speak, your opinion will take over your words and you will not be objective in your words.

Proverbs 16:26 ...the hungry mouth drives him on...

8. *What have my tendencies been in the past?*

9. *Am I believing this to get a benefit in my life or am I wanting to give and change?*

10. *Am I seeking to change according to God's will or am I seeking for God to line up with my will?*

Seeking twenty counselors to hear what you want to hear, is not seeking counsel. It is looking to legitimize the decision you have already made in your heart.

11. Is it going to benefit me or is it going to cost me?

King David was offered Arannah's threshing floor to make an offering to God for his error before God, but he refused to take it saying he would not give God something that didn't cost him something. It was a matter of valuing God, not merely offering a gift - 2 Samuel, chapter 24.

12. Do I have any preconceived ideas in this area?

The traditions of men, doctrines of men, bad experiences, false experiences, and other negative influences can affect your preconceived ideas in a matter. Knowing your weaknesses can protect you from failure in hearing God correctly in your present realities. When you have a problem in an area, don't go to someone who has a problem in the same area. Experience is not the best teacher. The Holy Spirit is. You can't comfort unless you have been comforted. Just having experience in an area doesn't qualify you to give answers. Having the authority and grace of God to give the solutions is the key to victory. If you have been married six times, the problem could be you. If you have had fifty jobs, the problem could be you. The voice of God will always send us in the direction of responsibility and it will not be a voice that endorses our running from things in life.

13. Do I have any blind spots, habits, or other areas that could hinder my perception?

This means, you might need to ask someone who knows you. Ask your spouse. Ask someone with authority in your life.

14. Is my perception clouded by any bitterness, unforgiveness, or any form of selfishness?

Mean people hear a mean God. Angry people hear an angry God. Promiscuous people hear a God without boundaries. Legalistic people hear a God of only law. What about the anti-church books? They are often reactions to something and they carry a bitter spirit, rather than a spirit of honor towards the church. They are often tainted by a bitter wound of something wrong and lack a spirit of love and faith for what is life.

15. *Am I wanting this because I am dissatisfied with what I have?*

Running from something is an illegitimate action; while being sent to something or sent upon a journey of faith is legitimate. How you leave a thing is how you will enter the next thing in life. I told God there were two places I would not live and those were the first two places He sent me in life. When I embraced loving those places He sent me to a place of instant love.

16. *Is it Scriptural to seek God in this matter or has God already forbidden it in His word?*

Illegitimate thoughts lead to illegitimate answers:
* I'm thinking about getting drunk tonight
* I'm thinking about committing fornication or adultery
* I'm thinking about not working
* I'm thinking about using drugs

17. *Is Faith my motivation or fear?*

The fear of God is not the fear of the stick. That is the fear of circumstances. Panic prayers, crisis instructions that involve a curse if you don't comply, chain letters with a promised blessing or a promised curse, or other words containing control or manipulation are not the voice of God. At best they are a perversion of something that God may have said. Most likely they are simply words of deception that carry burdens of bondage, condemnation, and shame.

18. *Do I sense the leading of the Holy Spirit or do I feel manipulated, controlled, or pushed out of guilt?*

Conviction that produces faith brings life, but conviction without faith is condemnation.

19. Do I have confidence that God will be proved as God or am I trying to prove that He isn't?

An example of proving God would be in His instructions of tithe. When God says to test Him with the tithe He did not mean test Him to see if it works or not. He meant to test Him with confidence that responding to Him with the spillover testimony of the prophetic tenth is a sure thing. We are to test Him to see that He is faithful, not to see if He is or not.

20. Am I willing to admit that I might be wrong?

James 3:17 says that the wisdom from God is willing to yield. When we are not willing to yield, it is not likely an instruction from God, unless we are being asked to renounce Christ or some other covenant commitment in life. When we hear God we may hear Him perfectly, but we usually don't fully understand its interpretation or its application initially. We must be willing to yield in the process of hearing Him.

21. Do I have two to three witnesses?

Two or three witnesses is not just in one day. It could be two or three solid witnesses in a process of time. Time is a friend of the witnesses in hearing God, not an enemy. The first 'go' is simply a word from God, there must also be a 'go' concerning the will of God, and a 'go' in the application of that word.

22. Am I afraid to seek a witness?

If you are afraid to seek a witness that is a good check that what you're hearing may not be God. God's voice inspires faith and it is grounded in a revelation of God's love. It is not filled with fear and is willing to be right or wrong in order to see what God wants fulfilled in one's life.

23. Do I have peace with God in all the areas of my life?

Am I in sin in any area of my life? This is simply asking, "Have I separated from God in any area?" The sin of discouragement is not being discouraged. It is rooted in some place of detachment. There is some form of gap between me and God, or me and others. I have taken an offense in some area and now I have become discouraged. I am living in a place of judgment and dependent upon mercy, when I should be living in a place of blessing and depending upon God's grace. When this happens it makes it difficult for me to hear God. I become tempted to see my future fulfilled through relationships of the flesh. I enter into the sin of Numbers chapter 25.

Choosing to be intimate with fleshly carnality can create a gap between God and us. It blinds us to the presence of God and doesn't allow God intimate access to our hearts as He desires. It will hinder us in hearing God. When this happens we must choose to reestablish our connection with God. God has not pushed us away, we have chosen to be intimate with something of the flesh rather than God, and now there is a stronghold of the flesh in our lives preventing us from hearing God clearly.

In Numbers chapter 25 we find a story of what happened to the Israelites when they fell for the scheme of the false prophet Balaam. He and King Balak conspired to tempt God's people to invite foreign gods into their lives through relationships with the daughters of their land.

Revelation 2:14 "But I have a few things against you, because you have there those who hold the doctrine of Balaam, who taught Balak to put a stumbling block before the children of Israel, to eat things sacrificed to idols, and to commit sexual immorality."

Instead of entering the Promised Land, they stopped at the Acacia Grove and worshipped the Baal of Peor. The Acacia Grove is the place of scourging and it is symbolic of the blood of the Cross. It is place that demands mercy, but it is not the throne of grace that transforms hearts and minds. It should be the place that represents no more gap between men and God, but by camping there the Israelites entered into fleshly relationships that invited the Baal of Peor. The name Peor means gap. They had created a gap between them and God by becoming intimate with fleshly things that were not part of their inheritance in God. It was there that they committed harlotry with the women of Moab. Moab was the son of the oldest daughter of Lot. He was conceived through an act of incest after the destruction of Sodom, when Lot's oldest daughter became pregnant by her drunken father because of her fear that there would be no future. Moab represents an incestuous seed of the flesh for fear of no future. Spiritually it is to produce a seed of self; to seek a future motivated by the nature of selfish flesh.

Numbers 25:1-3 Now Israel remained in Acacia Grove, and the people began to commit harlotry with the women of Moab. They invited the people to the sacrifices of their gods, and the people ate and bowed down to their gods. So Israel was joined to Baal of Peor, and the anger of the LORD was aroused against Israel.

The children of Israel had created a gap between them and God through a relationship with the flesh that symbolized an inheritance of self-seeking carnality, when they should have been moving forward into the land of the Promise. The children of Israel camped at the cross of judgment, rather than moving forward to the throne of grace.

Numbers 25:4-5 Then the LORD said to Moses, "Take all the leaders of the people and hang the offenders before the LORD, out in the sun, that the fierce anger of the LORD may turn away from Israel." So Moses said to the judges of Israel, "Every one of you kill his men who were joined to Baal of Peor."

The word of the Lord was simply to stop being intimate with those things that created a gap between them and God. The gap of the flesh had brought a judgment into the camp. It appears that an Israelite man and Midianite woman were caught in an act of intercourse at the door of the tabernacle of meeting. The Scripture reads that they were weeping at the door of the tabernacle. The word "weeping" is the Hebrew word "בָּכָה bākāh (HSRN 1058) a primitive root; *to weep*; generally *to bemoan.*" Phinehas, the son of Eleazar, the son of Aaron the priest, took a javelin and thrust both of them through, the man and the woman. His action implies the state of their relationship when he drove the spear through them both.

Numbers 25:6-8 And indeed, one of the children of Israel came and presented to his brethren a Midianite woman in the sight of Moses and in the sight of all the congregation of the children of Israel, who were weeping at the door of the tabernacle of meeting. Now when Phinehas the son of Eleazar, the son of Aaron the priest, saw it, he rose from among the congregation and took a javelin in his hand; and he went after the man of Israel into the tent and thrust both of them through, the man of Israel, and the woman through her body. So the plague was stopped among the children of Israel.

The name Midian means judgment. An act of fleshly carnality was bringing judgment into the camp. Phinehas stopped the judgment of the flesh by killing the act of the flesh without hesitation. Killing the act of the flesh brought peace back to the camp of Israel. Doing away with the act of the flesh reestablished the peace that God had given the people through His covenant of mercy. It reestablished a covenant of God's presence (grace) that could take them forward into the Promised Land.

Numbers 25:9-13 And those who died in the plague were twenty-four thousand. Then the LORD spoke to Moses, saying: "Phinehas the son of Eleazar, the son of Aaron the priest, has turned back My wrath from the children of Israel, because he was zealous with My zeal among them, so that I did not consume the children of Israel in My zeal. Therefore say, "Behold, I give to him My covenant of peace; and it shall be to him and his descendants after him a covenant of an everlasting priesthood, because he was zealous for his God, and made atonement for the children of Israel.' "

When we do something that creates a gap between God and us, the simple thing to do is to be like Phinehas. Choosing to execute the act of the flesh will reestablish the covenant of peace. Ceasing the act of the flesh closes the gap and empowers us to regain our access to God through His Spirit. In the New Covenant we have the power to end the flesh and indulge in the Spirit through at intimate relationship with God at the throne of grace (Heb. 4:16).

Peace with God in all areas of our lives includes the practical things of living according to godly principles. If we don't do our part, we cannot expect God to do His. There is a principle of binding and loosing. Whatever is loosed on earth is loosed in heaven. More specifically, certain things have been set to be loosed in heaven once they are loosed upon the earth. When Elijah needed water, he poured out water on the sacrifice and it returned as rain from heaven. As it is with rain, vapors ascend and then they return as rain upon the earth. Rain doesn't initiate in heaven, it begins as loosing vapors upon the earth. God has granted forgiveness to all people but, unless we loose forgiveness to others, God is bound from forgiving us.

Matthew 6:14-15 "For if you forgive men their trespasses, your heavenly Father will also forgive you. But if you do not forgive men their trespasses, neither will your Father forgive your trespasses.

Unless a husband honors his wife his prayers are hindered before God. God is ready to answer prayers, because answered prayers are an expression of honor from God to men. We must loose the ability for God to answer us by loosing honor on earth. Husbands must hear, understand, and respond to their own wives to loose God's ability to hear, understand, and respond to them from heaven.

1 Peter 3:7 Husbands, likewise, dwell with them with understanding, giving honor to the wife, as to the weaker vessel, and as being heirs together of the grace of life, that your prayers may not be hindered.

The husband is part of the bride of Christ and it is established in heaven that Jesus shows honor to His bride, but if a husband fails to honor his natural bride he hinders Jesus from honoring him upon the earth. Honor must be loosed in the earth for the blessing of pre-established honor to be released from heaven.

Angels are ministering spirits sent to those who inherit salvation, but there must be a loosing of angels upon the earth to receive the blessings that angels bring from heaven.

Abram's act of tithe to Melchizedek was a response to the gratuity of bread and wine (Gen. 14:18-23). He didn't have his goods in mind when he tithed to the King. He had the gifts of the King in mind. Abram didn't keep a stitch of the goods that he possessed. He knew that he needed all that God had in heaven for him to bring the testimony of heaven into his life upon the earth. If he was to be God's house in the earth then the food of God's house was necessary for him to become all that he was destined to be. His destiny in God was dependent upon his response to the flesh manifestation of Christ before his eyes. This demonstration of tithe from Abram's heart had nothing to do with any command that God had ever given. It was a revelation given to Abram by the Spirit of God when He encountered a manifestation of Christ upon the earth. It was a loosing on earth to receive the blessing pre-ordained from heaven. This is known as a tithe level relationship with God. The tithe is our response to God's giving of heavenly blessings.

When the gratuity of the Holy Spirit is given in our lives, a physical response empowered by the life of the Spirit from heaven looses the further blessings of heaven into our lives. The Holy Spirit is the earnest of all that is to be released in and through our lives from heaven.

A further account of loosing and binding was revealed through the life of Jacob (Gen. 28:10-22). When Jacob awoke from his dream he didn't say, "How awesome is God!" He said, "How awesome is this place!" He understood that he was in the place of the house of God. He was sleeping in the very place of destiny. The rock that he saw as a pillow needed to stand upright and be called what God saw it to be. A place that meant, *isolated* or *separated place* (Luz) needed to be called

– the house of God (Bethel). Jacob was not isolated or separated from God. He was the place of God's habitation. He understood that God was with him. He took the sleeping place and confirmed that it was truly a standing place, a place of inheritance. He took the rock that was a pillow and stood it upright as a pillar. He anointed the standing pillar with oil as a testimony to the place of the manifestation of Christ in the earth. There was an open heaven over his life and angels were ascending and descending. They were ascending from the house of God upon the earth to bring back all of the heavenly supply needed for that house to be known as the gate of heaven in the earth. Jacob didn't give the gratuity of tithe so that there would be an open heaven. He gave the tithe because he knew he was the gate of heaven. He didn't give the tithe so that God would bless his earthly possessions. He gave the tithe as a testimony to all that would come from heaven. He was responding to God, not invoking God to respond to him. He knew that God would keep him in his way and that way was the path of destiny set before him by God. God would rebuke the devourer on his behalf not because of what he did, but because of who he was. He responded with tithe because of who he was, not because of what God would do. He knew that God was the giver of bread and that there would be food in God's house, not the house of isolation or separation from God. His tithe was a testimony to his oneness with God. He had a covenant of peace with God and he knew that God would provide heavenly bread to change his character and to prove His will done in his life. He knew that God would clothe him and give him the outward evidence that would cause the nations to call him blessed. Jacob didn't tithe to get these things. He tithed because he knew that the gratuities of God would prove to lead to the full provision of the inheritance of God in his life. His act of tithe was a prophetic sign to his response to God. The test before him was not one to prove whether God could perform or not. It was a test that proved that God is who He says He is. Tithe was a response level testimony to the giving culture of God in His house. Being the place of the manifest presence of God in the earth looses angels to ascend and descend with the increased blessings of heaven. There must be a loosing on earth for there to be a pre-determined loosing in heaven. Angels are initiated from the house of God in the earth.

John 1:51 And He said to him, "Most assuredly, I say to you, hereafter you shall see heaven open, and the angels of God ascending and descending upon the Son of Man."

Tithe is a response level relationship whereby we respond to the bread and wine of Melchizedek with a prophetic tenth, declaring that the full inheritance of heaven is to be made known in God's house through the gate of heaven in the earth. It is like the submersion in the Holy Spirit, a holy testimony spills out from our hearts and submerges us in a testimony that declares we are a holy nation before God in the earth! We are dependent upon God as our righteousness and we are an earthly testimony of His peace, the evidence our oneness with Him in heaven while upon this earth.

24. Am I In rebellion in any way?

Has any God-given authority in my life instructed me to be obedient in an area and have I failed to do so? Has the Holy Spirit spoken to my heart in some way and I have not responded with obedience? That is rebellion and it will hinder me from hearing God clearly. I may hear the words that He is speaking, but I will twist His words in a way that results in my own destruction.

25. Do I have the inner peace of God in my heart?

The enemy can't fake that witness. It is the place of no gap between us and God. It is not the same as peace in your soul alone. You can have peace in your heart and be in conflict of soul. Abiding in the peace of your heart will bring peace to your soul.

26. If I look back at my life, is there a pattern that directs in the direction that I sense I am to take?

Our path in life is connected to who we are in life. The will of God doesn't come from what we want to do or what we think God wants us to do. Wisdom, the direction to the future, is connected to who we are. We are the will of God and the things we do in life are connected to who we are.

Proverbs 1:20-21 Wisdom calls aloud outside; she raises her voice in the open squares. She cries out in the chief concourses, at the openings of the gates in the city she speaks her words...

The New American Standard Bible uses the word 'street' for 'outside'. In these verses we see that wisdom is found in the street, in the open squares, in the chief concourses, and in the gates of the city. To understand these four things we must compare them to four small creatures described by Solomon in Proverbs chapter 30.

Proverbs 30:24-28 There are four things which are little on the earth, but they are exceedingly wise: The ants are a people not strong, yet they prepare their food in the summer; The rock badgers are a feeble folk, yet they make their homes in the crags; The locusts have no king, yet they all advance in ranks; The spider (or lizard) skillfully grasps with its hands, and it is in kings' palaces.

Wisdom is in the street; it is like an ant. The ant knows what season it is, it knows where it is in life by where it is in the journey of life. Is it winter? Is it summer? It doesn't need to be told by a commander, it knows where it is in the journey of life. What time is it? What is necessary today? There will be more to do tomorrow, but what is the present season of life?

Wisdom raises her voice in the open squares; it is like a rock badger in its quest to live. Though the rock badger is small and not considerably strong, it uses its natural environment to capture its food. It builds its home in the crags of the rocks, and uses its house as a place of protection and a way of surprising its prey to sustain itself in life. What is in the open squares that leads to my future? What is obviously around me and can serve me in my destiny of life?

Wisdom cries out in the chief concourses; it is like the locust. The locust realizes that if it lives in close relationship with other locusts it can

183

do impossible things. What relationships are in my life? How do those relationships serve the purpose of who I am? Who am I joined to? My direction forward is connected to the relationships given to me in life.

Wisdom speaks at the gates in the city; it is like a spider or a lizard. The spider or lizard are small, but they are faithful with what they can grasp hold of and they end up in influential places. Their influence in the city comes from their personal abilities. Those abilities are part of who they are and they are merely faithful with what is in front of them. What are my abilities and how am I being faithful today with what is directly in front of me? This will lead to my journey of influence in life.

God is not scattered in His strategies. Wisdom is found in the street. It is found in the continuity of the path that God has been leading me in. Wisdom is found in the environment I am suited for. It is found in the place where I can live. It is in the open square. Wisdom is found in relationships, my journey in life is connected to others. I am not to be alone. Wisdom is found through my abilities. It is not in something I am not created or equipped to do.

27. Is there an effectual door to enter through?

We must remember that when it comes to an open door or closed door request there are other necessary witnesses involved. As I have written, an open door doesn't necessarily mean it is the will of God, nor is a closed door alone an indication that something is not the will of God. Sometimes the open door is a test of our love for God and our honor in our covenants. Sometimes a closed door is intended to inspire our faith and patience in a matter. It is through faith and patience that the promises of God are inherited. Endurance is the number one testimony of something that is sent of God. It has the ability to last and to overcome.

28. Are there any special giftings or abilities needed to do this, and if so, do I have those giftings and abilities?

God will increase our abilities, anoint our abilities, challenge the sharpening of our abilities, or reveal our undiscovered abilities, but He will not call us to do anything we were not created to do. If we cannot sing, He will not call us to be a vocal artist. If we are not good at something it doesn't mean we are not good. It simply means we are good and best at something else. God's words to us will be consistent with our God-given abilities and destiny.

29. Does this matter merit the seeking of godly counsel, and if so, have I sought such?

If I am your pastor and you are buying a new car you don't need to call me. If you have a problem with debt and you are buying a new car you might need to call. If you are hearing God in an area of weakness in your life you need to have a witness that is not weak in that area.

30. If God has said this, is it God's timing?

31. Am I under authority, and am I operating under that authority, in this decision?

32. Do I feel like I'm going to die if I don't get this?

If you feel you are going to die if you don't get something or if what you think doesn't happen will be too much to bear, you are likely not hearing God correctly in some way. This is what led to the insurrection of Absalom in the day of David.

There is a story in 2 Samuel chapter 13. Jonadab was the nephew of King David. He convinced Amnon, David's son and half brother of Absalom, to take Absalom's sister Tamar and sexually defile her because he was lustfully sick for her. Amnon's illegitimate passions for Tamar had made him distressed to the point of sickness. Jonadab presented a scheme by which Amnon could seduce Tamar and Amnon thought that Jonadab's scheme was the thing to do (2 Sam. 13:1-14). After Amnon had dishonored Tamar, he hated her and put her away from him. Tamar's brother Absalom hated Amnon for what he had done and Tamar remained desolate in Absalom's house from then on. David did not deal with Amnon and Absalom hated Amnon and looked for an opportunity to get his revenge. Two years later Absalom invited the king's sons to Baal Hazor to receive the sheep shearing there. Absalom convinced David that his son Amnon should for sure come, even though it was known that Absalom despised him. Amnon went and Absalom had his servants kill Amnon while he was intoxicated at the feast. King David grieved the loss of Amnon with his other sons, but Absalom separated from David and his family and David did not see him for three years. David sought to return him home after three years and Absalom came home, but his relationship with his father was never restored. He held bitterness in his heart towards his father David for what had been done to his sister Tamar and how David had grieved over the death of Amnon, but had not sided with Absalom in the vindication for what he felt was justice. This was the set up for the insurrection of the kingdom by Absalom. Jonadab had set up Amnon to want what he could not have and this set a chain-reaction of other relationships that ended in the rebellion in the kingdom.

If you feel you're going to die if you don't get something or if something doesn't happen, it could be a set up for a chain-reaction of destruction in relationships concerning authority. It is best to be willing to yield and watch God bring His will to pass.

33. Am I willing to lay this down?

34. Have I reasoned this to be good?

If you've been arguing in your mind all day long whether something is God or not, chances are it is not God or there is something not quiet right yet in the word, will, or way of the matter.

35. Am I doing this because it seems like the only thing that will work?

The will of God is immeasurable in your life. You are not called to do one thing. You are called to be something and someone, therefore many things can be the revealed will of God in your life. If you feel that one thing is the only option you have, be careful. It may not be the will of God.

36. Do I feel that this will make me wise?

If you feel you will be a better person if you do this, it is not the pure voice of God. God says you are already the best. He is pleased with you because you are a son or a daughter of His, and His direction in your life won't make Him love you more. If you feel doing a certain thing will make you smarter, more important, more valuable, more loved, or anything beyond the identity of what you already are as a child of God, you are not hearing correctly.

37. Do I feel that I can be open with this decision or do I feel that I must conceal it?

Sometimes you keep secrets, but it can't be a pattern. God will never tell you something that you cannot share with those in authority in your life. Secrets alone create shadows and darkness and they are not the testimony of light.

38. Can I easily share this with those who are in authority in my life?

˙Concluding Prayer

I pray that this book has inspired you to hear the voice of Holy Spirit in your heart. I pray that hearing God will be the source of growing in intimacy with Him in your life. Let's not make hearing God a task or a job that has to be accomplished. Let's hear God as our Father, our Husband, our Helper, and our Friend. I pray that as you hear God you will grow in understanding who you were born to be. May all shame be lifted from your life as you receive increasing revelation of His love for you. It is through a revelation of His love that His voice will inspire faith in your heart. His words are life-giving words and His desire is to give you life in all things.

I pray that God will guide you as you learn the dance of relationship with Him in your life's journey. May He grant you the grace to overcome every hindrance to His voice. May you be a God-seeker, and not a word seeker. I pray you recognize His providential guidance and His specific words in your path in life. May His voice in your heart transform your character, nature, way, power, and authority to become those that are like God, your Father.

I pray that you will learn the significant witnesses to His voice. It is your relationship with Him that matters and He has been mapping out the witnesses of His voice in your heart all of your life. I pray that you will be sensitive to the witnesses of faith, peace, and all that is found in the fruit of His Spirit. May you rely upon the manifest presence of Christ within your spirit to discern His thoughts, intents, reasonings, imaginations, and emotions in your soul. I pray that you will learn to recognize the specific language that God uses with you in His communication to your heart. He is your Father and you are His child. It is that intimate!

I pray that you will discover the purpose of hearing God in your life. May it be the purpose of relationship with Him first and then with your covenant connections in life. May God use you to overcome the gates of hell by the power of His voice within you! May you be abundantly full of His life in your spirit, your soul, and all of your being. My desire is that you will discover a passionate, hungry attitude that breaks through every resisting wall to His voice in your life.

I also pray that you will not just hear God, but that you will be empowered to respond to Him in all things. May you increasingly realize that you are the will of God and that the things you do in life will be true to who God has made you to be. May the Spirit of revelation empower you to grow in knowing God's general will in life so you will also excel in His specific will for your life in every season of your life. May you understand His revelation, the interpretation of His revelation, and the application of His words in the various aspects and seasons of His continued guidance to your standing each day and your path to tomorrow.

Hearing God is a wonderful part of walking with Him. Don't make it a task or an obligation of obedience to some God you perceive to be angry or hard in His ways. Ask the correct questions that keep your heart and mind safe, but ask them from the perspective of being a child of God who is your Father and loves you very much. May God grant you the grace of hearing Him, knowing Him, and being who He has made you to be in this world for the glory of His name.

I ask these things in Jesus's Name, the One who knows how to hear God and respond to His will. He is a Son, thus His view of God is as His Father. He abides in the Father and the Father in Him, thus He knows the mystery of the fellowship of His Holy Spirit. May the substance of who He is be the substance of who you become. Please, enjoy the journey and dance the dance of life with God!